Prep-Ahead Meals
FROM SCRATCH

Alea Milham

Founder of the Food Blog Premeditated Leftovers

PAGE STREET
PUBLISHING CO.

First published in 2016 by

Page Street Publishing Co.

27 Congress Street, Suite 103

Salem, MA 01970

www.pagestreetpublishing.com

Distributed by Macmillan, sales in Canada by The Canadian Manda Group.

19   18   17   16   1   2   3   4   5

ISBN-13: 978-1-62414-204-8

ISBN-10: 1-62414-204-4

Library of Congress Control Number: 2015943524

Cover and book design by Page Street Publishing Co.

Photography by Chris Holloman

Cover Image: Getty Images

Printed and bound in China

Page Street is proud to be a member of 1% for the Planet. Members donate one percent of their sales to one or more of the over 1,500 environmental and sustainability charities across the globe who participate in this program.

Dedicated to military spouses who are busy
holding it all together on the home front.

Contents

INTRODUCTION

A friend once asked if I was interested in participating in a cooking challenge such as the television show *Chopped* because I liked cooking so much. I said, "Four random ingredients and 30 minutes to prepare an entrée? That doesn't sound like fun; that sounds stressful." Upon reflection, I realized that is what many of us are faced with on weeknights, only instead of judges we are trying to please our hungry kids. No wonder so many families resort to prepackaged foods and take-out.

On one of our cross-country moves, we arrived at our destination late and we were faced with more delays once we got there. We were all tired, hungry and grumpy. My husband suggested I feed the kids a quick snack of junk food. I responded through gritted teeth, "All I want to do is feed my family a nutritious dinner." Fifteen years later and my husband is still reminding me of those words! Sometimes I find his teasing amusing, occasionally I find it annoying, but those words are still true: I want to feed my family healthy dinners even when the circumstances make that goal difficult.

Numerous studies support the idea that eating dinner as a family has long-term benefits for children, but I can't be the only person who wonders whether it is still beneficial if you are stressed out and scolding children while trying to prepare a healthy meal.

Rockwell Painting vs. Reality: I had to put away my mental picture of what an ideal dinner as a family looked like and strategize ways to create stress-free meals that fit into our lifestyle.

One stress-reducing step I took was to adjust dinnertime to fit *my family's schedule.* I would love to have everyone at the dinner table at 6:00 p.m., but it is easier on my whole family if I admit that it is never going to happen and plan to serve dinner at a time that is less stressful for us all.

For me, just having a plan can reduce stress and temptation. When driving home from an activity at 6:00 p.m., it is tempting to give into my youngest son's request to stop for French fries. Knowing that I can pull dinner together in 15 minutes and being able to say, "We're having White Bean and Chicken Ranch Tacos tonight" makes it easier for me to say no without guilt and actually has a good chance of being positively received.

Dinner doesn't need to be complicated or time-consuming to be nutritious. Although I am willing to compromise on what time I serve dinner, I don't want to compromise on the quality of food I feed my family. Just because I want to make dinners with wholesome ingredients doesn't mean that all those ingredients have to be prepared in the hour before dinner is served. Instead, I batch cook some of the key ingredients in advance, so I can easily pull the precooked foods together with fresh produce to create a quick dinner.

If the cook is stressed, everyone picks up on it. The more meal prep you do in advance, the more relaxed you are in the kitchen, which translates into a more enjoyable meal for everyone.

In *Prep-Ahead Meals from Scratch,* I share batch-cooking techniques and simple recipes that can be made quickly and with minimal steps, so you can fit home-cooked dinners into your fast-paced lifestyle.

REDEFINING CONVENIENCE FOOD

The cost of buying packaged convenience foods adds up fast. Most of my married life, I prepared meals from scratch. On my husband's last deployment, I was at home with two children and another on the way. I started picking up things like packages of precooked chicken strips, boxed rice mixes and pre-sliced vegetables to save time on meals. Then one day, the "per unit" price caught my eye. Have you ever stopped to figure out how much a package of precooked chicken strips costs per pound? You will find that it usually costs more than $8.00 a pound. I decided right then that if I was going to spend $8.00 a pound on meat, I would rather spend it on better cuts of meat that I can prepare myself instead of processed meat.

My life didn't get any less busy, so I decided to start creating my own convenience foods one day a week. This meant that I could use the foods I prepared ahead of time in place of packaged foods on busy nights.

It isn't as difficult as you may think to make your own convenience foods. First you stock up on the basic building blocks of your recipes, such as meat, beans and rice. Then, you cook those staples in bulk and freeze them in usable portions.

You can also use individual spices to create your own seasoning mixes. These can be stored in an airtight container with your other spices and will keep for up to a year.

Pantry staples can be used to create your own dressings and sauces. Most homemade dressings can be made in less than five minutes and can be kept in the refrigerator for up to a week.

You probably already know that packaged foods often contain additives and preservatives. By making your own convenience items, you not only save money, but you also have complete control of the ingredients and can serve your family healthier foods.

BATCH COOKING

You need not equate batch cooking with once-a-month freezer cooking. While once-a-month freezer cooking falls under the umbrella of batch cooking, it isn't necessary to spend a whole day cooking and filling your freezer with precooked meals. Furthermore, batch cooking can be adapted to fit your kitchen tools, lifestyle and schedule.

I use batch cooking as a frugal way of creating my own convenience foods to help streamline dinner preparation. Cooking basic ingredients in bulk enables me to quickly create dinners with minimal prep time on busy weeknights. Instead of buying packaged rice mix and canned beans, I now reach into my freezer and pull out these precooked items as I need them in recipes.

You can adapt batch cooking to a time-pressured schedule. You might like to spend an hour or two on the weekend batch cooking meat, rice and beans for meals for the rest of the week. Or you could double up when you are cooking items like chicken and then use the extra meat in future meals. You could fit small bits of batch cooking into your day when you are cooking other items. For example, if a recipe calls for 1-cup (165-g) of cooked rice, you could cook 4-cups (660-g) and freeze the extra rice for future recipes.

At the beginning of each chapter, I will share how to batch cook a different main ingredient in several different ways, how to prep ingredients for future meals, and for how to store ingredients. This will allow you to choose batch-cooking methods that use the equipment you already have in your kitchen so you can fit it into your lifestyle with ease.

SPEED PREP TECHNIQUES

In addition to batch cooking meats, beans and rice, you can speed meal prep by using some of the following techniques.

Use kitchen scissors to:

- » Cut green onions, peppers and herbs.
- » Cut the florets off broccoli or cauliflower.
- » Cut meat into cubes or strips. Depending on your cooking method, you can do this before or after cooking meat.

Use a pizza cutter to quickly cut bread into cubes to make croutons.

Chop or dice potatoes ahead of time. Then store them in the refrigerator for 1 to 2 days in a bowl of water to prevent the cut potatoes from discoloring.

If you have a food processor, pull it out and make use of it to prep ingredients in bulk. Your food processor will not only help you save time, but if you use it to prep ingredients instead of buying prepackaged foods, it can help you save money.

Food processors can be used for:

» Shredding cheese. Then freeze it in 2-cup (240-g) portions. You can freeze shredded cheese for up to 4 months. In most recipes that call for shredded cheese, you can use cheese straight from the freezer.

» Dicing or chopping onions and celery. Store them in a plastic bag in the refrigerator for 1 to 2 days or in the freezer for up to a month.

» Slicing carrots and mushrooms. Store sliced carrots in a plastic bag with a moist paper towel to keep them from drying out. Store mushrooms in a ventilated container.

» Making bread crumbs. I find it is easier to get a fine crumb if you freeze your bread first.

Peeling vegetables is optional. I rarely peel potatoes, and I never peel tomatoes. Just skipping this step in food prep will save you time and increase the nutritional value of your recipes.

FOOD STORAGE TIPS

» Store your food in usable portions. If, for instance, you freeze 6 cups (990 g) of rice in the same container when you are not planning on using all the rice at the same time, you better have an ice pick! Instead, consider the portion size you will need for your meals and freeze it in appropriate quantities.

» Don't immediately freeze cooked food. Allow it to cool off for a little bit, so you don't raise the temperature of the freezer by putting hot food in it. This will also prevent condensation from forming inside your container so fewer ice crystals will form on your food. However, for food safety reasons, do not let the cooked food sit out for more than an hour before packaging it and freezing it.

» Remove the air from the container because air causes freezer burn. Squeeze as much of the air as you can from freezer bags. If you are freezing food in containers, lay a piece of parchment paper or plastic wrap on top of the food before you put the lid on it. That will reduce the amount of air that comes in direct contact with your food.

» Label your food before you freeze it. You may think you will remember the difference between diced bell peppers and diced jalapeño peppers, but after a month, you probably will not be able to tell them apart. You can use freezer labels, but masking tape works just as well. Be sure to include the date when you write the contents.

» An inventory list on your freezer door can help prevent food waste and also prevents you from making duplicate purchases. Write items down on your freezer inventory list as you add them to your freezer. Be sure to include the date you froze them. Scratch items off the list as you use them. This allows you to see at a glance what you have available for meals.

» It is easy for food to get lost in the freezer. You can avoid this by moving the older food to the front and placing the new items behind it, so you don't end up wasting food by leaving it in the freezer for too long.

PULLING IT ALL TOGETHER WITH MENU PLANS

When you are busy, it seems like you barely have time to cook dinner, let alone make a meal plan and shopping list. In reality, the busier you are, the more you may find you need a menu plan. Ultimately, it will save you time and money.

1. Look at your schedule for the week and determine how many people will be home each night for dinner and how much time you have each evening to devote to preparing a meal. This will allow you to plan meals that fit better into your schedule.

2. Take a look in your freezer, refrigerator and pantry to see what you already have available to create meals.

3. Decide which meals you have most of the ingredients for and start a shopping list for the ingredients you will need to complete those recipes.

4. Check your grocery store circulars to see whether there are some great deals on ingredients that you want to use as a foundation for a meal. Add those to your shopping list, then add any other items you need to complete those meals.

5. Once you have chosen the meals you want to make, create a list of any items that will need to be batch cooked. Then choose which day you want to serve each meal. Plan your batch cooking and more time-consuming meals on the days when you have more time and your quick and easy meals on your busiest weeknights.

NOTE: To get in and out of the grocery store faster, organize your grocery list with like items grouped together.

MONEY-SAVING SHOPPING STRATEGIES

When you start incorporating batch-cooking techniques into your cooking plan, you can save money by skipping packaged foods and shopping primarily from the perimeter of the store. Here are some more ways to save on your grocery bill.

» Check the circulars for the local grocery stores to find sales. If necessary, adjust your grocery budget so you can stock up on items that you commonly use when they are on sale. This may mean that the first week or two, you have to cut back in other areas until you find your groove.

» Plan your menu around items that are on sale and make sure you have a realistic plan for how you are going to use the items that you buy. If you stock up on organic dried beans when they are on sale, but they sit in your cupboard uncooked and uneaten, they are a waste of money.

» Use coupons and money-saving apps on your mobile device to save money on the things you need.

» Shop in the bulk food section. Most grocery stores do not have a minimum that must be purchased from their bulk food section. It is perfectly acceptable to only buy 1 or 2 ounces (28 or 56 g) of sesame seeds from the bulk bin if that is all you need.

» Buy in-season produce when possible. If there are vegetables you wish to buy that are not in season, consider buying them from the frozen food section.

» Make a shopping list and stick to it. There are so many temptations in the store. Don't fall for the marketing traps on the end caps. Making a commitment to stick to the items that you have on your list will help you say no to impulse buys. If you grocery shop at warehouse stores, it is especially important to put on the blinders of self-discipline. Take your list, go directly to the grocery section, pick up the items you need and proceed to the cash registers.

The recipes in this cookbook are either naturally gluten-free or include recommendations for gluten-free substitutions.

Quick and Easy Chicken

⟲

I love the versatility of chicken. While some may describe chicken meat as bland, I view the mild flavor as an asset. Chicken's mild taste is the perfect foundation for layers of added flavor. It is adaptable to almost any seasoning combination, so you can serve it a different way each night of the week without the risk of boring your family.

Chicken is already an affordable meat to cook with, but by utilizing batch-cooking techniques, you can stretch chicken and your grocery budget even further while saving time on busy nights.

Purchasing a whole chicken is the most affordable way to buy chicken, but because it takes approximately an hour to roast a chicken, it doesn't fit it into most weeknight schedules. With the exception of a lazy Sunday night chicken dinner, I batch cook whole chickens while doing other kitchen chores and then use the meat as a base for quick and easy meals throughout the week.

Boneless, skinless chicken breasts are easy to batch cook in a variety of methods, but I actually prefer cooking chicken thighs. Thighs contain a little more fat, which produces a moister, more flavorful final product to work with in recipes. Chicken thighs have the added advantage of being quite a bit less expensive than chicken breasts.

I like to batch cook chicken shortly after I come home from the grocery store, but you can store the meat in the refrigerator for up to 2 days before cooking it. If you can't cook your chicken within 2 days of buying it, then freeze it. You can freeze chicken pieces for up to 6 months and a whole chicken for up to a year. You should not thaw and refreeze raw meat. However, you can thaw frozen chicken, cook it, repackage it in airtight containers or freezer bags, and then freeze the cooked meat for up to 3 months.

Before batch cooking chicken, I decide how I plan to use the cooked meat because it helps me choose the best batch-cooking method for the recipes I plan to make. If I need shredded chicken, I use the slow cooker method, the pressure cooker method or the oven to batch cook the meat. If I will be making a stir-fry dish, then I usually use the stove top method to quickly seal in the juices in the individual bite-size pieces, but broiling also works quite well. For some recipes, the batch-cooking method doesn't matter. In those instances, I choose whichever method is convenient for me at the time.

HOW TO BATCH COOK CHICKEN IN A SLOW COOKER

The slow cooker is the most forgiving method for batch cooking chicken. You have a little wiggle room in the cooking time. Also, you do not need to add any liquid to the slow cooker when you cook chicken.

» Place the chicken in the slow cooker and sprinkle with Seasoned Salt* (page 183) and pepper.

» Place the lid on the slow cooker and then cook for the times listed below.

Cook 4 to 6 pounds (1820 to 2730 g) of chicken breasts or thighs for 4 to 5 hours on high or 7 to 8 hours on low.

Cook a whole chicken for 4 to 5 hours on high or 6½ to 8 hours on low. The chicken should be almost falling off the bone.

*Use gluten-free Seasoned Salt to make this gluten-free.

HOW TO BATCH BROIL CHICKEN BREASTS AND THIGHS

Broiling is one of the fastest ways to cook chicken pieces. I am a fan of broiled chicken, but you do have to pay attention and check it occasionally to make sure you do not overcook the chicken. Broiling chicken produces chicken that is somewhat crisp on the outside and tender on the inside. This method is ideal for chicken that you plan to cube or cut into strips, but it does not work well for creating shredded chicken.

» Preheat the oven's broiler and set the oven's rack 6 inches (15 cm) from the heat source. You can cover the broiler pan with foil to make cleanup easier if you wish.

» Brush or rub the chicken with olive oil and sprinkle with Seasoned Salt* (page 183) and pepper.

» Place the chicken pieces bone side up (or ugly side up if cooking boneless chicken) on a broiling pan.

» Broil the chicken for 4 to 6 minutes. Then flip the pieces over and broil for an additional 4 to 6 minutes, or until cooked through and the juices run clear.

» Let the chicken rest for 5 minutes. Then cut it into cubes or strips.

*Use gluten-free Seasoned Salt to make this gluten-free.

HOW TO BATCH ROAST WHOLE CHICKENS

You can use this method to cook an extra chicken while you are cooking a chicken for Sunday dinner or you can use it to roast two chickens at once to prep extra meat for future meals.

» Preheat the oven to 500°F (250°C, or gas mark 10). Place the rack in the lower third of the oven.

» Remove the neck and giblets, then pat the chicken dry with a paper towel.

» Place the chicken breast side up in a roasting pan or oven-safe skillet. Brush the chicken with olive oil. Dust the chicken with Seasoned Salt* (page 183) and pepper. If you are serving one of the chickens for dinner that night, sprinkle it with Poultry Seasoning Mix (page 186).

» Place the chicken in the oven and lower the temperature to 400°F (200°C, or gas mark 6). Cook for 50 to 60 minutes, or until it reaches a temperature of 165°F (74°C) in the thickest part of the thigh.

» Let the chicken rest for 5 minutes before carving. Remove the skin if you wish to shred the chicken.

*Use gluten-free Seasoned Salt to make this gluten-free.

HOW TO BATCH COOK CHICKEN ON THE STOVE TOP

This is the method I most often use to cook boneless, skinless chicken breasts. You can use this to quickly batch cook strips or cubes of chicken meat. The meat cooks quickly, sealing in juices. I use kitchen scissors to quickly cut the meat into the desired-size pieces before cooking.

- » Cut the excess fat from the chicken breasts or thighs.
- » Cut the chicken into bite-size pieces or thin strips.
- » Add 1 tablespoon (15 ml) of olive oil to a large skillet and heat over medium-high heat.
- » Add the chicken pieces to the skillet and cook until browned on all sides.
- » Lower the heat and cook for 4 to 5 minutes longer, or until the chicken is cooked through and the juices run clear.

HOW TO BATCH COOK CHICKEN IN A PRESSURE COOKER

I love cooking chicken in a pressure cooker. The pressure cooker quickly produces chicken so tender it can be carved with a fork. Be sure to familiarize yourself with your pressure cooker's manual to ensure you are using it properly.

- » Place the cooking rack in the bottom of the pressure cooker.
- » Add 1 cup (235 ml) of Chicken Broth* (page 191) or water to the pressure cooker (use 2 cups [470 ml] if your pressure cooker has a removable pressure regulator).
- » Set the whole chicken or chicken pieces on the rack.
- » Cook a whole chicken for 25 to 28 minutes at high pressure. Cook 3 pounds (1365 g) of chicken pieces for 9 to 10 minutes at high pressure.
- » Use the quick pressure release method to stop the cooking.

*Use gluten-free Chicken Broth to make this gluten-free.

HOW TO BATCH BAKE CHICKEN BREASTS AND THIGHS

For many people, baking chicken pieces is the cooking method that they feel most comfortable with. However, this method is most likely to produce dry meat, which might explain why some people do not enjoy chicken. To produce a moist baked chicken, you need to keep it covered while baking and cook it for a shorter time at a higher temperature.

- » Preheat the oven to 450°F (230°C, or gas mark 8).
- » Brush the chicken pieces with olive oil and sprinkle with Seasoned Salt* (page 183) and pepper.
- » Place the chicken pieces in a baking dish and cover with foil.
- » Place the chicken in the oven, lower the temperature to 400°F (200°C, or gas mark 6), and bake for 30 to 40 minutes, or until the chicken is cooked through and the juices run clear.

*Use gluten-free Seasoned Salt to make this gluten-free.

STORING THE COOKED CHICKEN

Place 2 cups (280 g) of cut or shredded chicken in airtight containers or freezer bags. Allow the meat to come to room temperature before placing it in the refrigerator or freezer. Store the cooked chicken for 3 or 4 days in the refrigerator or up to 3 months in the freezer.

Thaw frozen chicken in the refrigerator overnight. If you froze your meat in a microwave-safe dish, you can quickly thaw it in the microwave. If you are adding the chicken to a soup, stew or chili recipe, you can add it frozen and adjust the cooking time.

BUFFALO RANCH CHICKEN SQUASH BOATS

Serves: 4-6

BEST BATCH-COOKING METHOD: Slow Cooker ∽ Pressure Cooker ∽ Roasting

My family loves buffalo ranch chicken. I love finding a way to get them to willingly eat more vegetables. Cooking the buffalo ranch chicken in yellow squash instead of serving it on a hamburger bun is an easy way to get them to eat more vegetables. The spicy buffalo ranch sauce trickles down and adds flavor to the squash and the squash helps balance the heat of the chicken.

4 yellow squash (I prefer straight-neck squash)

1 cup (140 g) shredded cooked chicken

1 cup (165 g) cooked rice

2 stalks celery, finely chopped

2 green onions, thinly sliced, divided

½ cup (120 ml) Ranch Salad Dressing* (page 187)

1 ½ to 2 tbsp (23 to 30 ml) hot sauce*

½ cup (60 g) shredded mozzarella cheese

Use gluten-free Ranch Salad Dressing and gluten-free hot sauce to make this dish gluten-free.

Preheat the oven to 350°F (180°C, or gas mark 4). Grease a casserole dish.

Cut the squash in half lengthwise. Scoop out the seeds.

In a medium bowl, combine the shredded chicken, rice, celery, most of the green onions, ranch dressing and hot sauce.

Divide the buffalo ranch mixture among the hollowed-out squash halves.

Top the stuffed squash with the cheese and remaining green onion slices.

Place the squash in a greased casserole dish. Bake for 25 minutes.

PREP-AHEAD TIP: The buffalo ranch chicken stuffing can be made in advance and stored in the refrigerator for 1 or 2 days.

Serves: 4

CHICKEN MARSALA PIZZA ON A YEAST-FREE PIZZA CRUST

BEST BATCH-COOKING METHOD: Any

This yeast-free pizza crust is similar to flat bread in texture. It can be made start to finish in less than 20 minutes, so it is a great substitute for traditional pizza crusts on busy nights.

Pizza Crust

1½ cups (180 g) all-purpose flour*

1½ tsp (4 g) baking soda

½ tsp Seasoned Salt* (page 183)

1 tsp garlic powder

1 tsp onion powder

1 tsp parsley (optional)

½ cup (120 ml) water

1 egg, beaten

Pizza Topping

2 tbsp (28 g) butter

2 tbsp (16 g) cornstarch

1 cup (235 ml) Marsala wine or dry sherry

½ cup (120 ml) milk

1 tsp garlic powder

1 tsp onion powder

½ tsp Seasoned Salt* (page 183)

¼ tsp pepper

2 cups (140 g) sliced mushrooms

2 cups (280 g) cubed cooked chicken

1½ to 2 cups (180 to 240 g) shredded mozzarella cheese

1 green onion, thinly sliced

* To make this pizza gluten-free, replace the all-purpose flour with 1 cup (120 g) rice flour, ½ cup (60 g) tapioca flour, ¼ cup (30 g) potato starch and ¾ teaspoon xanthan gum. Also, use gluten-free Seasoned Salt.

Preheat the oven to 400°F (200°C, or gas mark 6) and grease a pizza pan.

To make the pizza crust, combine the flour, baking soda, salt and spices in a large bowl.

Add the water and egg to the flour mixture and stir until the ingredients are thoroughly combined and form a ball. Knead the dough in the bowl until it is smooth.

Spread the dough out on a greased pizza pan using your fingers. Create a thicker edge to hold the toppings on the pizza crust. Bake for 5 minutes.

While the pizza crust is baking, make the topping: Melt the butter in a skillet over medium heat.

Use a whisk to combine the cornstarch with the melted butter. Slowly add the Marsala wine to the butter mixture, whisking the entire time. Add the milk, garlic powder, onion powder, salt and pepper. Stir well. Add the mushrooms and increase heat to medium-high. Cook for 5 minutes. Add the chicken pieces to the mushrooms. Stir to coat.

After removing the pizza crust from the oven, top with the chicken Marsala. Sprinkle the cheese over the chicken and mushrooms. Top with the sliced onions.

Bake for an additional 10 minutes, or until the cheese has melted and just begins to brown.

PREP-AHEAD TIP: I usually make the chicken Marsala topping while the crust is baking, but it can be made in advance and stored in the refrigerator for 1–2 days if needed.

ASIAN CHICKEN PASTA SALAD

BEST BATCH-COOKING METHOD: Any

This has all the tastiness of an Asian chicken salad and a pasta salad rolled into one. The pasta absorbs the flavor of the Asian salad dressing, making for an especially delicious pasta salad.

Asian Salad Dressing

¼ cup (60 ml) rice vinegar

⅓ cup (80 ml) mild-flavored oil

1 tbsp (15 ml) sesame oil (optional)

¼ cup (60 ml) soy sauce*

2 tbsp (40 ml) honey

2 cloves garlic, pressed

2 tbsp (16 g) minced fresh ginger root

2 tbsp (16 g) sesame seeds

Pasta Salad

8 oz (227 g) rotini pasta*

2 cups (280 g) cubed cooked chicken

2 cups (240 g) sliced carrot

2 cups (140 g) broccoli florets

6 oz (168 g) snow peas

1 green onion, thinly sliced

Substitute gluten-free soy sauce and gluten-free pasta to make this recipe gluten-free.

To make the dressing, add the dressing ingredients to a cruet or jar with a lid. Shake vigorously to combine.

To make the pasta salad, cook the pasta according to the package directions.

Combine the chicken, carrots, broccoli, snow peas and onion in a large bowl. Pour ¼ cup (60 ml) of the dressing over the chicken and vegetables. Toss to coat.

When the pasta is done cooking, place it in a colander and run it under cold water until the pasta is cold. Drain the water and then add the pasta to the chicken and vegetables. Pour ½ cup (120 ml) of the dressing over the pasta. Toss to coat.

Chill the pasta salad for an hour or two before serving. If the noodles have absorbed all of the dressing, add the remaining dressing and toss to coat.

PREP-AHEAD TIP: You can make the dressing in advance and store it in the refrigerator for 3 to 5 days. You can also make the entire salad in advance and refrigerate it overnight. Just toss before serving to evenly coat the ingredients with the dressing.

CHICKEN FAJITA PIZZA WITH A CORNMEAL CRUST

BEST BATCH-COOKING METHOD: Any

Serves: 4

The hardest part of making pizza at my house is when I have hungry kids hovering while the pizza dough rises. That is why I am always looking for new ways to create pizza crusts that don't require yeast. This rustic pizza can be made in less than 20 minutes. The crust is made of cornmeal, eggs, cheese, water and spices, so you don't have to wait for the crust to rise.

Although this pizza is very easy to make, if you take a minute to artfully arrange the colorful pepper strips it will give it a wow factor, making it look like you worked much harder than you did.

Pizza Crust

2 cups (280 g) cornmeal

1 cup (235 ml) water

2 eggs, beaten

2 tsp (6 g) Taco Seasoning Mix* (page 184)

1 cup (120 g) shredded mozzarella cheese

Pizza Toppings

½ cup (120 g) salsa*

1 cup (140 g) cooked chicken strips

1 cup (120 g) bell pepper strips (you can use a variety of pepper colors)

¼ cup (40 g) sliced red onion

1 cup (120 g) shredded medium cheddar cheese

1 cup (120 g) shredded mozzarella cheese

* Use gluten-free Taco Seasoning Mix and gluten-free salsa to make this pizza gluten-free.

Preheat the oven to 400°F (200°C, or gas mark 6) and grease a pizza pan.

To make the crust, in a medium bowl, add the cornmeal, water, eggs and taco seasoning. Mix well. Add the cheese and stir until it is thoroughly mixed through the batter.

Spoon the pizza batter onto the greased pizza pan and press it into place using your fingers. Create a thicker edge to hold the toppings on the pizza crust.

Place the pizza pan in the oven and bake for 5 minutes.

For the toppings: Remove the pizza crust and top it with the salsa. Arrange the chicken strips, pepper strips and onion slices on top of the salsa. Sprinkle the cheeses over the top of the pizza.

Bake for 10 minutes longer, or until the cheese melts and begins to brown.

PREP-AHEAD TIP: The toppings come together very quickly, but you can speed the prep time by cutting the peppers and onions into strips the day before.

ASIAN CHICKEN AND RICE SOUP

BEST BATCH-COOKING METHOD: Any

Serves: 4

The soy sauce and ginger in this easy soup recipe lend a mild Asian flavor, creating a tasty twist on traditional chicken soup.

This recipe uses a few items that are not in most pantries, but if you pick up rice vinegar and mirin, you can use them to make a variety of Asian recipes at home. In the long run you could save money by creating your favorite Asian dishes at home instead of ordering out.

1 tbsp (15 ml) olive oil

¼ cup (40 g) diced onion

2 cloves garlic, minced

4 cups (940 ml) Chicken Broth* (page 191)

2 tbsp (30 ml) soy sauce*

¼ cup (60 ml) rice vinegar

1 tbsp (15 ml) mirin

1½ tsp (4 g) grated ginger

1½ cups (140 g) shredded cabbage

½ cup (65 g) julienned carrots

1 cup (120 g) diced cooked chicken

1½ cups (240 g) cooked rice

1 green onion, thinly sliced (optional)

Use a gluten-free soy sauce and gluten-free Chicken Broth to make this recipe gluten-free.

Heat the olive oil in a large pot. Add the onion and garlic and sauté until the onion is translucent.

Add the chicken broth, soy sauce, vinegar, mirin and ginger. Stir to combine. Add the cabbage and carrots. Cook over medium-high heat until the broth begins to boil.

Lower the heat and simmer for 8 minutes.

Add the chicken and rice and cook for 2 to 3 minutes, or until the rice and chicken are heated through. Serve immediately, garnished with green onion slices.

PREP-AHEAD TIP: You can dice the onion, julienne the carrots and shred the cabbage a day before making the soup. Store them in sealable plastic bags or lidded containers.

CHICKEN PARMESAN PASTA BAKE

BEST BATCH-COOKING METHOD: Any

This chicken Parmesan recipe has all the cheesy goodness of traditional chicken Parmesan, but cooks in a fraction of the time. Since the pasta is cooked in the same pan, you will have fewer dishes to clean after dinner.

1 (16-oz [455-g]) package rotini noodles*

3½ cups (823 ml) Spaghetti Sauce* (page 188), divided

2½ cups (590 ml) water

2 cups (240 g) cooked chicken strips

1½ cups (180 g) shredded mozzarella cheese

½ cup (50 g) grated Parmesan cheese

* Use gluten-free noodles and gluten-free Spaghetti Sauce to make this dish gluten-free.

Preheat the oven to 450°F (230°C, or gas mark 8).

Place the uncooked pasta in the bottom of a 12 x 9-inch (30.5 x 23–cm) casserole dish.

In a small bowl, combine 3 cups (705 ml) of the spaghetti sauce and the water. Pour the mixture over the pasta and stir to coat.

Cover the pan with foil and bake for 25 minutes.

Remove the foil and spread the chicken strips over the top of the pasta. Spoon the remaining ½ cup (123 ml) spaghetti sauce over the chicken. Sprinkle the cheeses over the top.

Place the pan back in the oven and bake for 10 minutes uncovered, or until the cheeses melt and the chicken is heated through.

PREP-AHEAD TIP: I make the spaghetti sauce (page 188) a day or two day ahead to reduce the prep time on this meal. You can also shred the cheese ahead of time and store it in a sealed container in the refrigerator for a week or in the freezer for 3 to 4 months.

CHICKEN ALFREDO STUFFED SHELLS WITH BROCCOLI

BEST BATCH-COOKING METHOD: Slow Cooker ∽ Pressure Cooker ∽ Roasting

This is pure comfort food! Instead of serving chicken Alfredo over noodles, I have stuffed it inside large pasta shells, creating an easy make-ahead dish.

Pasta Shell

18 large pasta shells*

2 cups (240 g) shredded chicken

2 cups (140 g) chopped broccoli

3 green onions, thinly sliced

1 cup (120 g) shredded mozzarella cheese

Alfredo Sauce

¼ cup (56 g) butter

2 tbsp (16 g) cornstarch

1 cup (235 ml) milk

1 cup (235 ml) Vegetable Broth* (page 193)

1½ cups (180 g) shredded mozzarella cheese

½ cup (50 g) grated Parmesan

2 tsp (6 g) garlic powder

1 tbsp (2 g) dried parsley

Pinch of pepper

* Use gluten-free pasta shells and gluten-free Vegetable Broth to make this dish gluten-free.

Preheat the oven to 350°F (180°C, or gas mark 4).

To make the pasta shells, cook the pasta shells according to the package directions.

While the pasta shells are cooking, combine the shredded chicken, broccoli, onion and cheese in a bowl.

To make the Alfredo sauce, melt the butter in a medium saucepot, and then add the cornstarch. Stir until smooth. Cook over medium-high heat until the mixture is smooth and bubbly, stirring constantly. Add the milk slowly, stirring until well blended. Add the broth, cheeses, garlic powder, parsley and pepper. Stir over medium heat until the cheese is melted and the sauce is smooth.

Add 1½ cups (355 ml) of the Alfredo sauce to the chicken mixture and stir to combine.

Spoon ¼ cup (60 ml) of the Alfredo sauce into the pan and spread over the bottom. Spoon the chicken mixture into the pasta shells and place the shells in the pan. Drizzle the remaining Alfredo sauce over the pasta shells.

Bake for 20 minutes, or until cooked through and bubbly.

PREP-AHEAD TIP: You can assemble the stuffed shells in advance if you wish. You can either refrigerate the stuffed shells overnight in the refrigerator or you can freeze them for up to 2 months in the freezer.

NOTE: Since this recipe only calls for 18 large pasta shells and most boxes of shells have 35 or more, this is a great recipe to double. You can make one for dinner and place the other one in the freezer for another time.

CAPRESE CHICKEN QUESADILLAS

BEST BATCH-COOKING METHOD: Slow Cooker ⁓ Pressure Cooker ⁓ Roasting

Serves: 4

I love the flavor of Caprese hors d'oeuvres, but rarely have an opportunity to indulge in them. Just because I don't spend much time at cocktail parties doesn't mean I can't enjoy the flavors at home by using the same ingredients to create quick and easy quesadillas.

Fresh basil is an essential ingredient in Caprese recipes. During the summer, I grow basil in my garden and during the winter I grow basil on the windowsill in my kitchen. The cost of one small basil plant is usually about the same price as buying a bunch of fresh basil from the produce section of your local grocery store, but the basil plant will continue to provide fresh leaves for months.

1 tbsp (15 ml) olive oil

16 small tortillas*

2 cups (240 g) shredded mozzarella cheese

1 cup (140 g) shredded cooked chicken

2 Roma tomatoes, thinly sliced

8 large basil leaves

Use gluten-free tortillas to make this dish gluten-free.

Preheat a large skillet over medium heat. Brush the pan with oil.

Place as many tortillas on the skillet as will fit. Sprinkle 2 tablespoons (16 g) of cheese on each tortilla. Place 2 tablespoons (18 g) shredded chicken on top of the cheese. Add 1 or 2 tomato slices and 1 large basil leaf. Top with 2 more tablespoons (16 g) of cheese. Place another tortilla on top and press it down to evenly distribute the ingredients between the tortillas.

Cook until the bottom tortilla is brown. Flip the quesadillas over using a large spatula and cook until the other tortilla is brown, 3 to 4 minutes on each side.

Repeat until all of your quesadillas have been made.

Cut in half and serve while hot.

PREP-AHEAD TIP: You can slice your tomatoes the night before and store them in a sealed container in the refrigerator.

CHICKEN CORDON BLEU RICE BAKE

BEST BATCH-COOKING METHOD: Any

This Chicken Cordon Bleu Rice Bake has all the flavors of Chicken Cordon Bleu, but can be made in half the time.

Sauce

3 tbsp (42 g) butter

2 tbsp (16 g) cornstarch

2 cups (470 ml) milk

1 tbsp (15 g) Dijon mustard*

¼ tsp dried basil

¼ tsp dried rosemary

Pinch of coarsely ground pepper

Topping

2 tbsp (28 g) butter, melted

¾ cup (90 g) Bread Crumbs* (page 190)

½ tsp dried rosemary

½ tsp dried basil

1 tsp dried parsley

Rice Bake

2 cups (330 g) cooked rice

1½ cups (180 g) cooked chopped chicken

4 to 6 oz (112 to 168 g) Swiss cheese, thinly sliced

1 cup (150 g) thinly sliced ham

Use gluten-free mustard and Bread Crumbs to make this recipe gluten-free.

Preheat the oven to 350°F (180°C, or gas mark 4). Grease an 8 x 8-inch (20 x 20-cm) casserole dish.

To make the sauce, melt the butter in a saucepan. Whisk the cornstarch into the butter until it is smooth and bubbly. Slowly add the milk while stirring. Cook over medium heat until it thickens. Add the mustard and spices and stir until thoroughly incorporated.

To make the topping, combine the melted butter, bread crumbs and spices in a bowl. Stir until the spices are evenly distributed through the bread crumbs.

To make the casserole, spoon the rice into the bottom of the casserole dish. Spread chicken pieces over the top of the rice. Spoon half of the sauce over the chicken. Then add a layer of cheese. Top the cheese with a layer of ham. Spoon the remaining sauce over the ham. Sprinkle the bread crumb topping over the top of the dish.

Bake for 20 minutes, until cooked through and bubbly.

PREP-AHEAD TIP: This casserole can be assembled ahead of time and stored in the refrigerator for 1–2 days before cooking.

WHITE BEAN
AND CHICKEN RANCH TACOS

BEST BATCH-COOKING METHOD: Slow Cooker ∾ Pressure Cooker ∾ Roasting

This is a fun twist on traditional tacos. I often stretch our grocery budget by replacing some of the meat in recipes with beans. Since beans are so mild and take on the flavors of the other ingredients, I find they work well as a meat substitute in spicy or flavorful dishes.

1¾ cups (437 g) cooked cannellini beans or other white bean

1 cup (140 g) shredded cooked chicken

4 tsp (8 g) Taco Seasoning Mix*
(page 184)

¼ cup (60 ml) Ranch Salad Dressing*
(page 187)

6 to 8 tortillas*

2 cups (140 g) shredded lettuce

1 cup (120 g) shredded cheddar cheese

2 Roma tomatoes, diced

1 green onion, thinly sliced

* Use gluten-free tortillas, Taco Seasoning Mix and Ranch Salad Dressing to make these tacos gluten-free.

In a small pot, combine the beans, chicken, taco seasoning and ranch dressing. Stir to combine.

Cook over medium heat until the chicken and beans are heated through.

Heat the tortillas in the microwave if necessary to make them more pliable.

Divide the chicken ranch mixture among the tortillas.

Top with the lettuce, cheese, tomato and onion slices.

PREP-AHEAD TIP: You can make the white bean and chicken ranch taco mixture in advance and store it in the refrigerator for 2 or 3 days or in the freezer for up to 3 months. You can also prep all the toppings 1 or 2 days in advance, except the tomato. Store the prepped toppings in small covered serving bowls. Then you can pull them out and quickly set up a taco bar on a busy weeknight.

HONEY MUSTARD CHICKEN SALAD WRAPS

BEST BATCH-COOKING METHOD: Any

Serves: 8

I love chicken salads, but for some reason chicken salads have gained the reputation as "grown-up food." To make this dish more appealing to the kids in my life, I have coated it in honey-mustard dressing. While many people consider chicken salad a luncheon staple, it is my go-to dinner of choice on busy nights.

The dressing on this chicken salad is flavorful enough that I add the salad directly to the wrap without spreading additional condiments on the tortilla.

Honey Mustard Dressing

⅓ cup (80 g) mayonnaise

3 tbsp (33 g) mustard*

3 tbsp (45 ml) honey

Filling

2 cups (280 g) diced cooked chicken

1 cup (150 g) diced apple

¼ cup (40 g) diced red onion

¼ cup (27 g) sliced almonds

1 celery stalk, thinly sliced

8 medium tortillas or wraps*

Use gluten-free mustard and tortillas to make this recipe gluten-free.

To make the dressing, combine the mayonnaise, mustard and honey in a small bowl.

To make the filling, combine the chicken, apple, onion, almonds and celery in a medium bowl.

Pour the dressing over the chicken salad. Stir to thoroughly coat.

If you have time, place the chicken salad in the refrigerator for 2 hours to let it chill.

Heat the tortillas in the microwave if necessary to make them more pliable.

Place ½ cup (60 g) of chicken salad in the center of each wrap. Fold the bottom up to cover the chicken salad. Fold one side of the wrap over the chicken salad, then roll to close up the wrap.

NOTE: Save money on nuts by buying them from the bulk food section of your grocery store instead of from the baking aisle. You can freeze nuts for up to 6 months in a resealable freezer bag.

PREP-AHEAD TIP: I make this chicken salad 1–2 days ahead of time, so all I have to do is add the chicken salad to the wrap and fold it closed. No cooking or reheating required.

CHICKEN AND ARTICHOKE BAKE WITH SPINACH

BEST BATCH-COOKING METHOD: Any

If you enjoy hot artichoke dip, you will love this casserole. Using frozen artichoke hearts will lower the cost of making this dish. Since frozen artichoke hearts are not marinated, all 12 ounces (340 g) of the product is comprised of artichoke hearts rather than a significant portion of it being liquid.

---

1 (10-oz [280-g]) package frozen spinach, thawed and drained

1 (12-oz [340-g]) package frozen artichoke hearts, thawed and drained

4 cups (660 g) cooked rice

2 cups (280 g) diced cooked chicken

1 cup (120 g) shredded cheddar cheese, divided

1 cup (120 g) shredded mozzarella cheese

8 green onions, thinly sliced

½ cup (120 g) sour cream or plain yogurt

½ cup (120 g) mayonnaise

1 tsp garlic powder

Pinch of salt and pepper

Preheat the oven to 350°F (180°C, or gas mark 4). Grease a 12 x 9-inch (30.5 x 23-cm) casserole dish.

Squeeze all of the liquid from the spinach and artichoke hearts.

In a large bowl, combine the spinach, artichoke hearts, rice, chicken, ½ cup (60 g) of the cheddar cheese, mozzarella cheese, most of the green onions (save some for the top of the casserole), sour cream, mayonnaise and spices. Stir until all of the ingredients are thoroughly combined.

Spread the mixture into the greased casserole dish. Top with the remaining ½ cup (60 g) cheddar cheese and onion slices.

Bake for 25 minutes, or until the cheese melts and the casserole is heated through.

PREP-AHEAD TIP: This dish can be made ahead and stored in the refrigerator for up to 2 days or in the freezer for up to 2 months.

MANGO-GLAZED CHICKEN AND VEGETABLES

BEST BATCH-COOKING METHOD: Stove Top ∿ Broiled

Serves: 4

One day when I was shopping for apricot fruit spread, I noticed mango fruit spread for the same price as for apricot. Mangoes are a lot more expensive in my area than apricots are, so I realized that this was a way I could add mango flavor to recipes without spending a lot of extra money. You can use another flavor of jam or fruit spread in place of the mango fruit spread if you wish.

This recipe calls for grated ginger rather than dried ginger. Instead of buying fresh ginger every time I want to make a recipe that calls for fresh ginger, I buy a large root and freeze it. Each time a recipe calls for grated ginger, I pull out my frozen ginger root and grate it while it is still frozen and then put it back in the freezer until the next time I need it for a recipe.

---

1 tbsp (15 ml) olive oil

1 tbsp (15 ml) sesame oil

2 green onions, thinly sliced

2 cloves garlic, minced

1 cup (120 g) ¼-inch (6-mm)-thick sliced carrot

2 cups (150 g) snow peas

2 tsp (6 g) grated ginger

⅓ cup (80 g) mango fruit spread or jam

¼ cup (60 ml) water

2 tbsp (30 ml) soy sauce*

2 cups (280 g) cubed cooked chicken

2 cups (330 g) cooked rice

* To make this gluten-free, use a gluten-free soy sauce or coconut aminos in place of the soy sauce.

Add the oils, onion and garlic to a large skillet and sauté for 1 minute.

Add the carrot and continue sautéing for 3 minutes.

Add the snow peas and ginger and sauté for 5 minutes.

In a small bowl, combine the mango fruit spread, water and soy sauce.

Move the vegetables to the side of the pan and pour the mango mixture into the center of the skillet. Stir the mixture as the jam melts. Once the sauce is smooth, add the chicken. Toss to coat the chicken and vegetables with the mango glaze. Cook for 2 to 3 minutes longer, or until the chicken is heated through.

Serve over rice.

PREP-AHEAD TIP: This easy stir-fry comes together quickly, but you can reduce the prep time by slicing the onions and carrots ahead of time and storing them in a sealed container in the refrigerator for 2 or 3 days.

MEDITERRANEAN CHICKEN FRITTATA

BEST BATCH-COOKING METHOD: Any

Don't be put off by the long list of ingredients; many of them are just spices. This frittata comes together quickly. It is also a very flexible recipe, so if you don't have one of the vegetables, substitute something that you have available. Don't have artichoke hearts? Add zucchini instead.

1 tbsp (15 ml) olive oil

½ cup (80 g) diced onion

4 cloves garlic, minced

1 cup (300 g) frozen artichoke hearts, thawed and quartered

3 Roma tomatoes, diced

1 cup (140 g) cubed cooked chicken

¼ cup (25 g) sliced olives, plus extra for garnish

8 eggs, beaten

1½ tsp (1.5 g) oregano

1 tsp basil

1 tsp parsley

¼ tsp thyme

¼ tsp rosemary

Pinch of pepper

½ cup (60 g) shredded mozzarella cheese

Preheat the oven to broil.

Add the olive oil, onion, garlic, artichoke hearts and tomatoes to a 10-inch (25-cm) oven-safe frying pan. Cook over medium-high heat for 5 minutes, or until the onion is tender and the artichokes are heated through.

Add the chicken and olives and cook for an additional 2 minutes, or until the chicken is heated through.

Add the eggs to a small bowl and beat with a fork or an eggbeater. Add the spices to the eggs and mix well. Pour the eggs over the vegetable mixture. Cook over medium-low heat until the eggs are almost set, 4 to 5 minutes.

Remove the pan from the heat. Sprinkle the cheese over the top and spread remaining olive slices over the top.

Place the frying pan 4 to 6 inches (10 to 15 cm) beneath the broiler. Broil for 2 to 4 minutes, or until the eggs are cooked through and beginning to brown on top.

PREP-AHEAD TIP: You can dice the onions, slice the olives and shred the cheese 2 or 3 days in advance. You can also dice the Roma tomatoes the night before. Store the prepped vegetables in a sealed container in the refrigerator.

PINEAPPLE TERIYAKI CHICKEN

Serves: 4

BEST BATCH-COOKING METHOD: Stove Top ⌒ Broiled

When my kids were young, my mother-in-law made them pineapple teriyaki chicken legs whenever we went over for a barbecue. My kids loved her chicken so much that I incorporated the pineapple juice and teriyaki sauce from her recipe to create an easy chicken dish that I can quickly prepare on the stove top.

1 (14-oz [392-g]) can pineapple chunks, pineapple juice reserved

¼ cup (60 ml) teriyaki sauce*

¼ cup (60 ml) water

1 tbsp (8 g) cornstarch

1 tbsp (15 g) brown sugar

2 cups (280 g) diced cooked chicken

2 cups (330 g) cooked rice

* Use gluten-free teriyaki sauce to make this dish gluten-free.

Add ½ cup (120 ml) of the pineapple juice, teriyaki sauce, water and cornstarch to a skillet. Use a whisk to stir until the cornstarch is fully incorporated.

Add the brown sugar and cook over medium heat for 3 minutes, or until the sauce is thick and bubbly.

Add the chicken and pineapple chunks. Stir to coat. Cook over medium-low heat for 5 minutes, or until the chicken is heated through.

Serve over rice.

PREP-AHEAD TIP: The dish can be made in advance and stored in the refrigerator for 2 or 3 days. Reheat over medium-low heat before serving.

CHICKEN PAPRIKASH

BEST BATCH-COOKING METHOD: Any

Serves: 4

Grocery stores do not carry a lot of different varieties of paprika in the United States, so if you want authentic Hungarian paprika you have to order it online. I usually just use paprika ahumada, which is a sweet smoked paprika that is often sold as smoked paprika in grocery stores. If you would like to add a little heat to this dish, you can add a pinch of cayenne.

1 (12-oz [340-g]) package egg noodles*

2 tbsp (28 g) butter

1 cup (160 g) onion strips

¼ cup (35 g) diced red bell pepper

2 tsp (6 g) cornstarch

¾ cup (180 ml) Chicken Broth* (page 191)

4 tsp (12 g) smoked paprika

½ tsp garlic powder

2 cups (280 g) diced or strips cooked chicken

2 tbsp (30 g) sour cream

* Substitute gluten-free noodles and gluten-free Chicken Broth to make this dish gluten-free.

Cook the egg noodles according to the package directions.

While the egg noodles are cooking, melt the butter in a skillet. Add the onion and red pepper and cook for 5 to 7 minutes, or until the onion is tender and beginning to brown.

Remove from the heat and move the onion and peppers to the side of the pan. Stir the cornstarch into the butter until it is smooth. Slowly add the broth and stir well, mixing the onions and peppers back into the sauce.

Place the skillet back over medium heat and add the spices and chicken. Cook for 5 minutes, or until the chicken is heated through.

Add the sour cream and cook for 2 minutes.

Drain the egg noodles. Serve the chicken over the cooked noodles.

PREP-AHEAD TIP: You can cut the onion into strips and dice the peppers ahead of time. Store them in a sealed container in the refrigerator for 2 or 3 days or in the freezer for up to 3 months.

EASY CHICKEN CACCIATORE WITH CHEESE RAVIOLI

BEST BATCH-COOKING METHOD: Any

This is an easy one-dish dinner recipe. Instead of cooking pasta in a separate pot, I add frozen cheese ravioli in the last step of this recipe. The ravioli cooks while the sauce is simmering. This not only saves time but also the cheese in the pasta adds another layer of flavor to this classic dish.

1 tbsp (15 ml) olive oil

1 cup (160 g) diced onion

1 cup (150 g) bell pepper strips

2 cups (140 g) sliced mushrooms

4 cloves garlic, minced

1¾ cups (315 g) diced tomatoes or 1 (14.5-oz [406-g]) can diced tomatoes

1¾ cups (430 ml) or 1 (15-oz [430-ml]) can tomato sauce

2 tsp (2 g) basil

2 tsp (2 g) oregano

2 cups (280 g) cubed cooked chicken

2 tsp (8 g) sugar

Pinch of salt and pepper

16 oz (455 g) frozen cheese ravioli*

* Use gluten-free ravioli to make this dish gluten-free.

Heat the olive oil in a large skillet over medium-high heat. Add the onion, bell pepper, mushrooms and garlic to the skillet. Cook for 5 minutes, or until the vegetables are tender.

Stir in the diced tomatoes, tomato sauce, basil, oregano and chicken. Add the sugar, salt and pepper to taste.

Bring to a boil. Reduce the heat to medium-low, add the frozen ravioli and simmer for 8 minutes, or until the ravioli is heated through.

PREP-AHEAD TIP: You can dice the onions, cut the bell pepper and slice the mushrooms ahead of time and store in the refrigerator for 2 or 3 days.

APPLE, CRANBERRY AND CHICKEN SALAD WITH CRANBERRY VINAIGRETTE

BEST BATCH-COOKING METHOD: Any

This salad combines the sweetness of apples and dried cranberries with savory onions and bacon bits to satisfy both your appetite and your palate.

Cranberry Vinaigrette

½ cup (120 ml) mild-flavored oil such as safflower oil

¼ cup (60 ml) sweetened cranberry juice

¼ cup (60 ml) red wine vinegar

2 tsp (2 g) dried mustard

2 tsp (8 g) sugar

¼ tsp onion powder

¼ tsp garlic powder

¼ tsp pepper

Salad

6 to 8 loosely packed cups (420 to 560 g) salad greens

1 cup (140 g) diced cooked chicken

1 large sweet apple, cored and diced

½ cup (60 g) dried cranberries

½ cup (55 g) sliced almonds

2 green onions, thinly sliced

¼ cup (30 g) blue cheese crumbles (optional)

2 slices cooked bacon (page 47), crumbled (optional)

To make the vinaigrette, add the vinaigrette ingredients to a cruet or lidded jar. Shake well to mix.

To make the salad, divide the salad greens among 4 plates.

Top the greens with the chicken, apple pieces, cranberries, sliced almonds, green onions and blue cheese crumbles. Drizzle the dressing over the salads and top with the bacon bits.

NOTE: To save money on blue cheese, I buy the store's brand of blue cheese crumbles instead of buying a wedge from the deli section.

PREP-AHEAD TIP: The dressing can be made ahead of time and stored in the refrigerator for 3 to 5 days. You can also tear the salad greens and place them in a bowl. Place a paper towel on the top of the salad bowl before you cover it to keep your salad from wilting.

CHICKEN TETRAZZINI STUFFED PASTA SHELLS

Serves: 6

BEST BATCH-COOKING METHOD: Slow Cooker ↝ Pressure Cooker ↝ Roasting

My husband's aunt introduced me to my first tetrazzini, which is a poultry and mushroom dish served over pasta. She made her tetrazzini with leftover turkey the day after Thanksgiving. I enjoyed her recipe so much that I started making extra chicken throughout the year just so I could use it to make chicken tetrazzini. When I don't have enough shredded chicken to make a whole casserole dish of tetrazzini, I stretch it by stuffing it into large pasta shells instead.

18 large pasta shells*

2 tbsp (28 g) butter

1 cup (160 g) diced onion

½ cup (75 g) diced bell pepper

2 stalks celery, finely chopped

3 cloves garlic, minced

2 cups (140 g) finely chopped mushrooms

3 tbsp (24 g) cornstarch

1½ cups (355 ml) Chicken Broth* (page 191)

1½ cups (355 ml) milk

2 tsp (2 g) oregano

2 tsp (2 g) thyme

Pinch of Seasoned Salt* (page 183) and pepper

2 cups (280 g) shredded cooked chicken

1 cup (120 g) shredded cheddar cheese

1 cup (120 g) shredded mozzarella cheese

* Use gluten-free pasta shells, Chicken Broth and Seasoned Salt to make this dish gluten-free.

Preheat the oven to 350°F (180°C, or gas mark 4). Grease a 12 x 9-inch (30.5 x 23-cm) baking pan.

Cook the pasta shells according to the instructions on the box.

While the pasta is cooking, melt the butter in a skillet. Add the onion, bell pepper, celery and garlic and sauté until the onion is translucent. Add the mushrooms and sauté for 1 minute.

In a small bowl, whisk together the cornstarch and broth. Add the broth to the skillet. Add the milk and spices. Cook while stirring until the sauce thickens.

In a large bowl, combine the chicken and cheeses. Add all but 1½ cups (355 ml) of the mushroom sauce to the chicken mixture.

Spoon the chicken mixture into the cooked pasta shells. Place each filled shell in the greased casserole dish. Spoon the remaining mushroom sauce over the filled shells. Cover and bake for 15 minutes. Uncover and bake for 10 more minutes.

PREP-AHEAD TIP: To speed the prep time, you can chop the onions, bell pepper, celery and mushrooms 2 or 3 days in advance. You can also shred the cheese ahead of time.

CAJUN CHICKEN AND PASTA

BEST BATCH-COOKING METHOD: Any

You can transform a basic skillet recipe just by changing up the spices. My family thoroughly enjoys Cajun-spiced food, so I revamped a simple chicken and pasta skillet recipe just by seasoning it with Cajun Seasoning mix.

Serves: 4–6

1 tbsp (15 ml) olive oil

1 cup (160 g) diced onion

1 cup (150 g) diced red bell pepper

2 cloves garlic, minced

2 cups (470 ml) Vegetable Broth* (page 193), divided

1 cup (235 ml) water

8 oz (227 g) rotini pasta*

2 cups (280 g) cubed cooked chicken

2 Roma tomatoes, diced

2 tsp (4 g) Cajun Seasoning Mix* (page 183)

* Use gluten-free pasta, Vegetable Broth and Cajun Seasoning Mix to make this dish gluten-free.

Add the olive oil to a large skillet and heat over medium-high heat until hot. Add the onion, bell pepper and garlic; cook for 2 to 3 minutes, or until lightly browned.

Add 1¾ cups (410 ml) of the vegetable broth, water and pasta to the skillet and bring to a boil. Reduce the heat, cover and simmer for 6 to 8 minutes, or until the pasta is al dente.

Add the chicken, tomatoes, Cajun spice mix and remaining ¼ cup (60 ml) vegetable broth to the skillet. Stir until the spice mix is thoroughly incorporated.

Cook over medium-low heat for 2 minutes, or until the chicken is heated through.

PREP-AHEAD TIP: Dice the onions and red pepper ahead of time and store in a sealed container in the refrigerator for 2 or 3 days or in the freezer for up to 3 months.

Tasty Pork on a Budget

Next to chicken, pork is one of the most inexpensive meats you can buy. At regular price, it is lower than beef and when on sale it can rival chicken. Like chicken, pork is also quite versatile. It is compatible with the seasonings in a wide variety of cuisines, so don't be afraid to experiment with it.

You can expect to regularly find good sales on pork loin, pork shoulder roasts and hams. You can save even more by buying a whole or half pork loin and then cutting it into smaller roasts and pork loin chops and freezing it for future use.

In general, I use dry cooking methods, like roasting and broiling, for any cuts that contain the word loin and wet cooking methods like slow cooking for cuts that come from the shoulder. I only reheat whole hams for special occasions. Rather than serving large slices of ham with side dishes, I stretch my grocery budget by using diced or shaved ham in recipes to add flavor.

I usually try to batch cook raw pork shortly after I come home from the grocery store, but raw pork can be stored in the refrigerator for up to 2 days before cooking it. If you can't cook your raw pork within 2 days of buying it, then freeze it. You can freeze pork for up to 6 months.

Before I batch cook the pork, I make a list of the recipes I am planning to make with the cooked pork. This ensures I have cooked meat in the form I need it to prepare my recipes. If I need shredded pork, I use the slow cooker method, the pressure cooker method or roast it in the oven. If I will be making a stir-fry dish, then I use the stove top method or I broil it to quickly seal in the juices. If it doesn't matter which method I use for the recipe, then I choose whichever method is most convenient for me.

A cooked ham can be stored in the refrigerator up until its use-by date. It isn't advised that you freeze a whole cooked ham because it can affect the quality and the texture; however, ham that has been cut into cubes or slices does quite well in the freezer. Once you have opened the packaging on the ham, you should use it or freeze it within 5 days.

Do not thaw and then refreeze raw meat. However, you can thaw frozen pork, cook it, repackage it in airtight containers or freezer bags, and then freeze the cooked meat for up to 3 months.

HOW TO BATCH COOK PORK IN A SLOW COOKER

The slow cooker is ideal for making pulled pork. I like to use a shoulder roast like Boston butt in the slow cooker.

» Place your roast in the slow cooker and sprinkle with Seasoned Salt* (page 183) and pepper.

» Place the lid on the slow cooker and cook a 3- to 4-pound (1365- to 1820-g) roast on high for 6 to 8 hours, or until you can pull it apart with a fork.

*Use gluten-free Seasoned Salt to make this gluten-free.

HOW TO BATCH BROIL PORK CHOPS

Broiling is a fast and effective way to seal in the moisture and produce tender pork chops. The cooking time will vary depending on the thickness of the meat. Very thick pork chops can take up to 12 minutes on each side. To make cleanup easier, you can cover your broiling pan with foil if you wish.

» Preheat the oven's broiler and set the oven's rack 6 inches (15 cm) from the heat source.

» Brush or rub the pork chops with olive oil and sprinkle with Seasoned Salt* (page 183) and pepper.

» Place the pork chops on a broiling pan.

» Broil for 8 to 12 minutes, then flip and broil for 8 to 12 minutes on the other side, or until cooked through and the juices run clear.

» Let the pork rest for 5 minutes, then cut it into cubes or strips.

*Use gluten-free Seasoned Salt to make this gluten-free.

HOW TO BATCH COOK PORK ON THE STOVE TOP

This is the method I most often use to cook pork for stir-fries and stews. You can use this method to quickly batch cook strips or cubes of pork. The meat cooks quickly, sealing in juices. First, use a knife to cut a 2- to 3-pound (910- to 1365-g) roast into ½- to 1-inch (1.3- to 2.5-cm) thick "steaks." Then use kitchen scissors to quickly cut the meat into the desired size pieces. You can also use this method with pork chops.

» Cut the pork into bite-size pieces or thin strips.

» Add 1 tablespoon (15 ml) of olive oil to a large heated skillet.

» Add the pieces of meat to the skillet and cook over medium-high heat until browned on all sides.

» Lower the heat and cook for 4 to 5 minutes longer, or until the pork is cooked through and the juices run clear.

HOW TO BATCH COOK PORK IN A PRESSURE COOKER

Be sure to familiarize yourself with your pressure cooker's manual to ensure you are using it properly.

» Place the cooking rack in the bottom of the pressure cooker.

» Add 1 cup (235 ml) of Vegetable Broth* (page 193) or water to the pressure cooker (use 2 cups [470 ml] if it has a removable pressure regulator).

» Set the meat on the rack.

» Cook a 3-pound (1365-g) pork roast for 50 to 55 minutes at high pressure. Cook 2 pounds (910 g) of pork chops for 9 to 11 minutes at high pressure.

» Remove the pressure cooker from the heat source and allow it to sit as the pressure is naturally reduced. Do not attempt to open until all the steam has been released.

*Use gluten-free Vegetable Broth to make this gluten-free.

HOW TO BATCH COOK PORK ROASTS IN THE OVEN

I only use this method of cooking pork roasts if I am already making a pork roast for Sunday dinner or a special occasion. If cooking multiple pork roasts, do not let them touch while cooking so they will cook evenly. Try to choose roasts of similar size to cook together, so the cooking time will be about the same. Pull out the smallest roast when it is done and check the other roasts at 10-minute intervals.

» Preheat the oven to 500°F (250°C, or gas mark 10). Place the rack in the lower third of the oven.

» Place the pork roast fat side up in a roasting pan or oven-safe skillet. Brush with oil. Dust with Seasoned Salt* (page 183) and pepper.

» Place the pork roast in the oven and cook for 10 minutes.

» Lower the temperature to 200°F (100°C) and cook for 25 minutes per pound (455 g) or until it reaches a temperature of 145°F (63°C) in the thickest part of the roast.

» Let the roast rest for 5 minutes before carving. Slice what you need for dinner and then let the roast cool before you cut it into cubes or shred it for use in other meals.

*Use gluten-free Seasoned Salt to make this gluten-free.

HOW TO COOK BACON IN THE OVEN

I seriously debated whether to include bacon in any of the recipes in this cookbook, because bacon is quite expensive when compared to other cuts of pork. My oldest son made a passionate case for its inclusion, and obviously I caved.

I only buy bacon when I find a great sale. Then I stock up and buy enough to get us through until the next sale. I freeze the bacon until I need it, then I thaw it in the refrigerator overnight. I cook it in 2-pound (910-g) batches in the oven. We each enjoy a couple of pieces, then I crumble the bacon and freeze it until I need it to add flavor to a recipe. I usually add the frozen bacon directly to the dish because it thaws very quickly.

» Do not preheat your oven!

» Cover two large raised-edge baking sheets with foil.

» Spread 1 pound (455 g) of bacon slices on a baking sheet without touching. Repeat for another pound (455 g) of bacon.

» Place the bacon in the oven and set the temperature at 400°F (200°C, or gas mark 6).

» Bake for 15 to 20 minutes, or until it is brown and crispy. Watch it carefully during the last couple of minutes to make sure it doesn't burn.

» Remove the bacon from the pan and place it on a paper towel to remove the grease.

» Once the bacon has cooled to room temperature, freeze it in usable portions.

Note: You can save the bacon fat for future use. Pour it through cheesecloth to remove the impurities. Store it in the refrigerator. You can use the lard in place of oil in recipes to add extra flavor to dishes.

Bacon is used in 15-Minute "Baked" Beans (page 137), Ham and Cauliflower Casserole (page 64), Skillet Beef Burgundy (page 103) and Apple, Cranberry and Chicken Salad (page 41).

STORING COOKED PORK

Place 2 cups (300 g) of cubed or shredded pork in airtight containers or freezer bags. Allow the meat to cool before placing it in the refrigerator or freezer. Store cooked pork for 3 or 4 days in the refrigerator or up to 3 months in the freezer. Thaw frozen pork overnight in the refrigerator. If you freeze your meat in a microwave-safe dish you can quickly thaw it in the microwave. If you are adding the meat to a soup, stew or chili, you can add it frozen and adjust the cooking time.

CHIPOTLE PULLED PORK TACOS

BEST BATCH-COOKING METHOD: Slow Cooker ∽ Pressure Cooker ∽ Roasting

Serves: 4

For many years, I made tacos every Tuesday night for dinner. How did I keep my family from getting bored when I made tacos every single week? By changing up the meats and the seasonings used to flavor the tacos. Want more ideas for your taco night? Try White Bean and Chicken Ranch Tacos (page 30) or Lentil and Rice Tacos (page 134).

Having themed nights can make menu planning much easier, even if the themes are very general, such as pasta night or pizza night.

2 cups (300 g) pulled pork

½ cup (125 g) tomato sauce

2 tsp (6 g) Chipotle Seasoning Mix* (page 185)

1¾ cups (438 g) cooked black beans

8 tortillas*

2 cups (140 g) salad greens

1 cup (180 g) diced tomatoes

1 cup (120 g) shredded cheese

* Use gluten-free tortillas and gluten-free Chipotle Seasoning Mix to make this dish gluten-free.

Combine the pulled pork, tomato sauce, chipotle seasoning mix and black beans in a medium pot.

Cook over medium heat until the pork is heated through.

Heat the tortillas in the microwave for 1 minute if you wish.

Divide the pulled pork mixture among the tortillas.

Top with the salad greens, tomatoes and cheese.

PREP-AHEAD TIP: This chipotle pulled pork and bean mixture can be made in advance and stored in the refrigerator for up to 2 days or frozen for up to 3 months.

SKILLET MAC & CHEESE WITH HAM AND BROCCOLI

Serves: 4

For many families, packaged mac and cheese is a go-to meal on busy nights, but it really only takes a few extra minutes to make mac and cheese from scratch on the stove top. Cooking macaroni and cheese from scratch gives you complete control over the ingredients and allows you to avoid preservatives and food dyes while creating a more flavorful dish.

If you want to make this faster, cook the noodles in a separate pot while you start the sauce in a skillet. If you don't want to deal with extra dishes, cook the pasta in the skillet and then make the cheese sauce while the pasta is draining in a colander.

8 oz (227 g) elbow noodles*

2 tbsp (28 g) butter

¼ cup (40 g) diced onion

2 tbsp (16 g) cornstarch

½ tsp Seasoned Salt* (page 183)

Pinch of pepper

1½ cups (355 ml) milk

1 cup (120 g) shredded mild cheddar cheese

1 cup (120 g) shredded Monterey Jack cheese

½ cup (75 g) diced ham (optional)

1 cup (70 g) finely chopped broccoli (optional)

* Use gluten-free pasta and Seasoned Salt to make this dish gluten-free.

Cook the noodles according to the package directions. Drain and set aside.

Melt the butter in the same pot. Add the onion and sauté for 2 minutes.

Stir in the cornstarch, salt and pepper. Cook while stirring until smooth and bubbly.

Slowly add the milk while continuously stirring.

Add both cheeses and stir while cooking over medium-low heat until melted and completely incorporated.

Add the cooked noodles, ham and broccoli. Stir to coat. Cook over low heat until the ham is heated through, 2 to 3 minutes.

PREP-AHEAD TIP: You can dice the onions and cut the broccoli florets into small pieces 1 or 2 days in advance and store them in the refrigerator in small resealable bags.

HONEY LEMON PORK AND BROCCOLI

BEST BATCH-COOKING METHOD: Stove Top ‿ Broiled

Serves: 4

This quick and easy recipe has a bright, zesty flavor. It comes together in about 15 minutes, but if you want to speed up prep time, cut your broccoli florets the night before. After chopping your broccoli, place it in a bowl and cover with a moist paper towel to keep it from drying out.

Don't toss your broccoli stems! Peel the outside layer and then cut them into matchstick thin strips and use them to make broccoli slaw or use them in a stir-fry.

2 tbsp (30 ml) olive oil

4 cloves garlic, minced

4 cups (280 g) broccoli florets

½ cup (120 ml) Vegetable Broth* (page 193)

1 tbsp (8 g) cornstarch

3 tbsp (45 ml) lemon juice

4 tbsp (60 ml) honey

2 tsp (6 g) grated ginger

¼ tsp crushed red pepper flakes

2 cups (300 g) cubed cooked pork

2 cups (330 g) cooked rice

* Use gluten-free Vegetable Broth to make this dish gluten-free.

In a skillet, heat the oil over medium heat and sauté the garlic for 1 minute.

Add the broccoli and sauté for 3 minutes.

In a small bowl, whisk together the broth and cornstarch. Add the lemon juice, honey, ginger and red pepper flakes.

Add the honey lemon sauce and pork to the skillet. Stir to coat the broccoli and pork.

Simmer for 4 minutes, or until the pork is heated through and the sauce has thickened.

Serve over rice.

NOTE: To save money, pick up extra lemons when they are on sale. Squeeze the lemon juice and measure by the tablespoon (15 ml) into ice-cube trays. Once the lemon juice cubes are frozen, store them in a resealable freezer bag and use them in recipes that call for fresh lemon juice.

PREP-AHEAD TIP: You can cut the broccoli into florets 1 or 2 days in advance and store them in a large sealable bag in the refrigerator.

SKILLET SCALLOPED POTATOES WITH HAM AND PEAS

Serves: 4

Scalloped potatoes are one of my favorite dishes from my childhood. However, I rarely made it for my kids because it took over an hour to prepare. I realized that I could save time if I didn't peel the potatoes, but that only sped up the prep time. Then one day I had the idea of making scalloped potatoes on the stove top and discovered I could make them start to finish in about 25 minutes.

1 tbsp (14 g) butter

1 cup (160 g) onion strips

6 medium red potatoes, thinly sliced

⅔ cup (160 ml) Vegetable Broth* (page 193) or water

1 tsp basil

¼ tsp Seasoned Salt* (page 183)

Pinch of pepper

1 tbsp + 2 tsp (14 g) cornstarch

1½ cups (355 ml) milk

1 cup (150 g) diced ham

1 cup (130 g) frozen peas, thawed

* Use gluten-free Vegetable Broth and Seasoned Salt to make this gluten-free.

Heat the butter in a large skillet. Add the onions and cook over medium heat until the onions are tender and just beginning to brown.

Spread the potatoes over the onions. Pour the broth over the potatoes and cook over medium heat until the broth begins to boil, 2 to 4 minutes.

Lower the heat, sprinkle the spices over the tops of the potatoes, put a lid on the skillet and cook for 5 minutes. After 5 minutes, flip the potatoes over. Cover again and cook until the potatoes are fork-tender, 3 to 5 minutes.

In a small bowl, whisk the cornstarch and a ¼ cup (60 ml) of the milk together. Slowly add the remaining milk while whisking continuously to remove any lumps.

Add the ham, peas and milk mixture to the potatoes. Cook uncovered over medium-low heat until the sauce thickens and the ham and peas are heated through, approximately 5 minutes.

PREP-AHEAD TIP: You can cut the onions and potatoes 1 or 2 days in advance if you wish. Store the onions in a sealed container. Store the potato slices in a bowl, covered with water.

WHITE CHILI WITH RICE

BEST BATCH-COOKING METHOD: Slow Cooker ∽ Pressure Cooker ∽ Roasting

Chili is always a hit with my family. This white chili recipe is a refreshing alternative to red chili recipes. It is very flavorful but not overly spicy, making it a good choice for those who do not enjoy "hot" foods.

1 tbsp (15 ml) olive oil

1 cup (160 g) diced onion

4 cloves garlic, minced

1 stalk celery, diced

3 cups (705 ml) Chicken Broth* (page 191) or Vegetable Broth (page 193)

3½ cups (875 g) cooked white beans

2 cups (300 g) shredded cooked pork

2 cups (330 g) cooked rice

1 cup (130 g) frozen corn

1 (4.5-oz [125-g]) can mild green chiles

1 tsp ground cumin

1 tsp oregano

⅛ tsp ground red pepper

* Use gluten-free broth to make this dish gluten-free.

Heat the oil in a large pot over medium heat. Add the onion, garlic and celery and sauté for 5 minutes, or until the onion is tender.

Add the broth, beans, pork, rice, corn, green chiles and spices.

Cook over medium-high heat until it reaches a boil. Lower the heat and simmer for 10 minutes, or until heated through.

PREP-AHEAD TIP: This chili can be made ahead of time and stored in the refrigerator for 2 or 3 days or in the freezer for up to 3 months.

ASIAN PORK AND VEGETABLE FRITTATA

BEST BATCH-COOKING METHOD: Any

Just because frittatas contain eggs doesn't mean they should be limited to breakfasts and brunches. The mild flavor of eggs makes them a great base for this Asian inspired frittata. The speed with which a frittata can be cooked makes them an ideal dinner for busy nights.

1 tbsp (15 ml) olive oil

3 green onions, thinly sliced

2 cloves garlic, minced

2 tsp (6 g) grated ginger

½ cup (120 g) julienned carrots

½ cup (115 g) finely chopped cauliflower

1 cup (70 g) finely chopped broccoli

½ cup (75 g) diced red bell pepper

1 cup (150 g) diced cooked pork roast

8 eggs

2 tbsp (30 ml) soy sauce*

1 tbsp (8 g) sesame seeds

Substitute a gluten-free soy sauce to make this recipe gluten-free.

Preheat the oven to broil.

Add the oil, onions, garlic, ginger, carrots, cauliflower, broccoli and pepper to a 10-inch (25-cm) oven-safe frying pan.

Cook over medium-high heat for 4 to 5 minutes, or until the vegetables are almost fork-tender.

Add the diced pork to the vegetable mixture. Cook for 1 minute, or until the pork is heated through.

Add the eggs and soy sauce to a small bowl and beat with a fork or eggbeater. Pour the egg mixture over the vegetables and pork.

Cook over medium-low heat until the eggs are almost set, 4 to 5 minutes.

Sprinkle the sesame seeds over the eggs. Place the frying pan 4 to 6 inches (10 to 15 cm) beneath the broiler. Broil for 2 to 4 minutes, or until the eggs are cooked through and beginning to brown.

Cut into wedges and serve immediately.

PREP-AHEAD TIP: You can cut the onion, pepper and carrots 2–3 days ahead of time.

CRUSTLESS HAM AND ASPARAGUS QUICHE

Serves: 6

I am not sure how quiche got the reputation for being difficult, but it is undeserved. Quiches are actually quite easy to make. And if you make your quiche without a crust it is not only easy but also fairly quick to prepare.

1 cup (150 g) diced ham

1 cup (70 g) thinly sliced asparagus

½ cup (60 g) shredded Swiss cheese

4 eggs

1 cup (235 ml) milk

½ tsp garlic powder

½ tsp onion powder

Pinch of salt and pepper

Preheat the oven to 400°F (200°C, or gas mark 6). Grease a deep-dish pie pan.

Spread the ham, asparagus and cheese evenly inside the pan.

Add the eggs to a large bowl and beat them with a whisk. Add the milk and spices and continue to whisk until thoroughly combined. Pour the egg mixture over the ham and asparagus.

Bake for 30 to 35 minutes, or until the quiche has set.

PREP-AHEAD TIP: You can slice the asparagus 1 or 2 days in advance and store it in a sealed container in the refrigerator.

WHITE BEAN AND HAM SOUP WITH SPINACH

This bean soup is comforting and delicious in its simplicity. Instead of using flour to thicken the broth, I mash 1 cup (250 g) of beans. This provides a thick base without creating a heaviness to the broth.

3½ cups (875 g) cooked cannellini beans or other white beans, divided

1 tbsp (15 ml) olive oil

1 cup (160 g) diced onion

2 cloves garlic, minced

1 celery stalk, thinly sliced

4 cups (940 ml) Vegetable Broth* (page 193)

1 tsp oregano

½ tsp basil

¼ tsp thyme

¼ tsp Seasoned Salt* (page 183)

Pinch of pepper

1½ cups (275 g) diced ham

2 cups (140 g) fresh spinach

Use gluten-free Vegetable Broth and Seasoned Salt to make this dish gluten-free.

Mash 1 cup (250 g) of the cooked beans.

Heat the olive oil in a large pot. Add the onions, garlic and celery to the pot. Sauté the vegetables until the onions are translucent, approximately 5 minutes.

Add the mashed beans, broth and spices to the pot. Cook over medium-high heat until it reaches a boil. Lower the heat and simmer for 5 minutes.

Add the ham and spinach and cook until the spinach is wilted and the ham is heated through.

PREP-AHEAD TIP: Although this soup comes together in under 20 minutes, you can speed dinner even more by making it ahead of time. It can be stored in the refrigerator for 2 or 3 days or in the freezer for 3 months. Reheat over medium-low heat.

POTATO, HAM AND CORN CHOWDER

This hearty chowder recipe comes together in less than 30 minutes, though the herbs add layers of flavor, making it seem like you put much more time into it.

2 tbsp (28 g) butter

1 cup (160 g) diced onion

2 stalks celery, thinly sliced

2 cloves garlic, minced

2 tbsp (16 g) cornstarch

2½ cups (590 ml) milk, divided

3½ cups (820 ml) Vegetable Broth* (page 193)

2 cups (240 g) diced potato

1 tsp basil

½ tsp thyme

½ tsp sage

¼ tsp rosemary

¼ tsp Seasoned Salt* (page 183)

Pinch of pepper

2 cups (300 g) diced ham

2 cups (260 g) frozen corn

* Use gluten-free Vegetable Broth and Seasoned Salt to make this chowder gluten-free.

Melt the butter in a large pot. Add the onion, celery and garlic and sauté until the onions are translucent, approximately 5 minutes.

Stir in the cornstarch. Slowly add 1 cup (235 ml) of the milk while continuously stirring. Add the remaining 1½ cups (355 ml) milk and vegetable broth. Stir well to ensure there are no lumps.

Add the potato and spices and cook over medium heat until it reaches a boil. Lower the heat and simmer for 10 minutes.

Add the ham and corn and cook for an additional 5 minutes.

PREP-AHEAD TIP: You can make this ahead of time and keep it in the refrigerator for up to 3 days or store it in the freezer for up to 3 months. Rewarm over low heat.

HAM AND CAULIFLOWER CASSEROLE

Serves: 6

Don't be put off by the cauliflower in the recipe; it is serious comfort food even though the main ingredient is a vegetable. Cauliflower's mild flavor allows it to take on the flavors of the other ingredients.

I have sprinkled a little bacon over the top of this casserole, but it isn't necessary. My oldest son disagrees, and you have him to thank for the inclusion of bacon not only in this recipe but also in this cookbook.

2 tbsp (28 g) butter

1½ cups (240 g) diced onion

4 cloves garlic, minced

1 head cauliflower, cut into small florets

¼ tsp coarsely ground pepper

2 cups (260 g) frozen corn, thawed and patted dry

2 cups (300 g) diced ham

1¼ cups (150 g) shredded mild cheddar cheese, divided

1¼ cups (150 g) shredded Monterey Jack cheese, divided

2 pieces cooked bacon (page 47), crumbled (optional)

Preheat the oven to 350°F (180°C, or gas mark 4).

Melt the butter in a large oven-safe skillet. Add the onion and garlic and sauté for 1 minute.

Add the cauliflower florets, sprinkle with pepper and sauté for 5 minutes.

Add the corn, ham, 1 cup (120 g) of the cheddar cheese and 1 cup (120 g) of the Monterey Jack cheese. Stir well to mix the ingredients. Sprinkle the remaining ¼ cup (30 g) cheddar cheese, the remaining ¼ cup (30 g) Monterey Jack cheese and the crumbled bacon over the top of the cauliflower mixture.

Bake for 20 minutes.

PREP-AHEAD TIP: You can dice the onion and shred the cheese ahead of time. You can also chop the cauliflower into small florets a day in advance and store in a sealable plastic bag in the refrigerator.

CARNITAS QUESADILLAS

Serves: 4

When I make pulled pork, I like to save some of the meat to make carnitas. Carnitas can be served in a variety of ways, including on their own, in tacos, on tostados and my favorite: in quesadillas.

I often make a double or triple batch of carnitas so we can enjoy them in many different dishes. If you want to make a large batch of carnitas, triple the recipe, place the meat on a large baking sheet and broil for several minutes, until the meat is a deep brown and crunchy on top.

---

2 cups (300 g) shredded pork

2 tbsp (30 ml) orange juice

2 tbsp (30 ml) water

½ tsp cumin

½ tsp oregano

½ tsp chili powder

½ tsp garlic powder

½ tsp onion powder

½ tsp smoked paprika

¼ tsp cinnamon

¼ tsp ancho chile powder

2 tbsp (30 ml) olive oil

16 corn tortillas*

2 cups (240 g) shredded mozzarella cheese

2 jalapeños, seeded and thinly sliced

* Use gluten-free tortillas to make this dish gluten-free.

In a medium bowl, combine the shredded pork, orange juice, water and spices. Stir until completely mixed together.

Heat the oil in a large skillet. Evenly distribute the shredded pork in the pan. Press it down so more of the meat is in contact with the surface of the skillet. Cook over high heat until the bottom side of the pork is golden brown and crusty. This only takes a couple of minutes, so watch it carefully.

Preheat a large frying pan or an electric skillet. Grease with oil right before making your quesadillas.

Top a tortilla with 2 tablespoons (16 g) of cheese. Add ¼ cup (38 g) of the carnitas. Sprinkle a few jalapeño slices over the meat. Top with 2 more tablespoons (16 g) of cheese and another tortilla.

Place the quesadilla on a greased skillet and cook until the bottom tortilla is brown. Flip and cook until the other tortilla is brown, 3 to 4 minutes on each side.

Repeat until all of your quesadillas have been made. Cut in half and serve while hot.

PREP-AHEAD TIP: You can make the carnitas ahead of time and store them in a sealed container in the refrigerator for 2 or 3 days.

PORK ALFREDO SKILLET WITH SPRING VEGETABLES

BEST BATCH-COOKING METHOD: Any

Serves: 6

My family loves pasta Alfredo. When I don't want to mess with washing extra pots and pans, I make it all in one skillet. It is usually made with chicken, but pork's flavor is mild enough that it works in this easy one-dish dinner.

When my kids were young they didn't care for Parmesan cheese, so I made Alfredo sauce entirely with mozzarella cheese. Because mozzarella cheese is usually quite a bit less expensive than Parmesan, it is not only a kid-friendly alternative but also a frugal substitution.

1 (16-oz [455 g]) package rotini pasta*

2 tbsp (28 g) butter

3 cups (705 ml) Vegetable Broth* (page 193)

2 cups (470 ml) milk

2 tsp (6 g) onion powder

2 tsp (6 g) garlic powder

1 tsp basil

½ tsp Seasoned Salt* (page 183)

Pinch of pepper

2 cups (260 g) thinly sliced carrots

2 cups (260 g) frozen peas

2 cups (300 g) diced cooked pork

1 cup (120 g) shredded mozzarella cheese

1 cup (100 g) grated Parmesan cheese

Use gluten-free pasta, Vegetable Broth and Seasoned Salt to make this dish gluten-free.

Add the pasta, butter, broth, milk, onion powder, garlic powder, basil, salt and pepper to a large skillet. Cook over medium-high heat until it reaches a boil.

Lower the heat, add the carrots and cover. Simmer for 10 minutes.

Add the frozen peas, cover again and simmer for 5 more minutes, or until the pasta is al dente.

Stir the pork and cheese into the pasta. Cook over low heat for 1 to 2 minutes, or until the cheese is melted and the pork is heated through.

PREP-AHEAD TIP: You can shred the cheese and slice the carrots ahead of time. Store the cheese in a sealed container for 4 or 5 days in the refrigerator or up to 3 months in the freezer. Store the carrots for 2 or 3 days in a sealed container with a moistened paper towel to keep the sliced carrots from drying out.

TUSCAN PORK

BEST BATCH-COOKING METHOD: Any

Tuscan pork chops are a traditional Italian dish. I enjoy the flavors of the dish, but we rarely eat whole pork chops. Instead of coating pork chops with the sauce, I simplified the process and stretched the pork further by adding pieces of pork to the rustic Tuscan red sauce and served it over linguini.

1 (8-oz [227 g]) package linguini*

1 tbsp (15 ml) olive oil

1 cup (160 g) diced onion

4 cloves garlic, minced

1½ cups (270 g) diced tomatoes

¼ cup (60 ml) Vegetable Broth* (page 193)

1 tbsp (15 ml) balsamic vinegar

1 tsp sugar

1 tbsp (3 g) oregano

2 tsp (2 g) basil

1 tsp thyme

1 bay leaf

2 cups (300 g) diced cooked pork

* Use gluten-free pasta and Vegetable Broth to make this dish gluten-free.

Cook the linguini according to the directions on the package.

While the linguini is cooking, heat the oil in a skillet. Add the onion and garlic and sauté for 5 minutes, or until the onion is tender.

Add the tomatoes, broth, vinegar, sugar and spices. Stir to combine the ingredients.

Add the pork and stir to coat. Cook over medium heat until it reaches a boil. Lower the heat and simmer for 10 minutes.

Remove the bay leaf before serving. Serve over the cooked linguini.

PREP-AHEAD TIP: You can cook the sauce ahead of time and keep it in the refrigerator for 2 or 3 days or freeze it for up to 3 months.

Serves: 4

BARBECUE PULLED PORK STUFFED SWEET POTATOES

BEST BATCH-COOKING METHOD: Slow Cooker ⤴ Pressure Cooker ⤴ Roasting

So many foods are more fun when stuffed in a potato skin including pulled pork!

4 medium sweet potatoes

3 cups (450 g) pulled pork

1 cup (250 g) Barbecue Sauce*
(page 189)

½ cup (60 g) shredded cheddar cheese

1 green onion, thinly sliced

Use gluten-free Barbecue Sauce to make this dish gluten-free.

Preheat the oven to 400°F (200°C, or gas mark 6).

Pierce the sweet potatoes with a fork and place on a baking sheet. Bake for 45 minutes, or until fork-tender.

When the sweet potatoes are ready, pull them from the oven, cut a small oval in the top of each potato and scoop out the sweet potato.

In a small bowl, combine the pulled pork and barbecue sauce.

Divide the pulled pork among the sweet potatoes. Top the stuffed sweet potatoes with the cheese and onion slices.

Place the sweet potatoes back in the oven and bake for 15 minutes, or until cheese is melted.

NOTE: You can turn the unused portion of sweet potatoes into Savory Mashed Sweet Potatoes (page 151), use as a topping for Chili Pie (page 89), or use in Black Bean and Sweet Potato Burritos (page 132).

PREP-AHEAD TIP: It takes a while to bake sweet potatoes, so I usually bake them the day before and store them in the refrigerator overnight. Sometimes I stuff them and have them ready to go the night before, and other times I wait and scoop out the sweet potatoes and fill them right before dinner.

CAJUN PULLED PORK WRAPS

BEST BATCH-COOKING METHOD: Slow Cooker ∽ Pressure Cooker ∽ Roasting

Serves: 8

Wraps are a busy mom's best friend. Because I rely on wraps on busy nights, I don't want my family to get bored, so I am always creating new flavor combinations. I use homemade Cajun Seasoning Mix (page 183) to flavor both the pulled pork and the mayonnaise to create a tasty spread for the wrap.

2 cups (300 g) pulled pork

¼ cup (65 g) tomato sauce

3 tbsp (45 ml) water

1 tbsp (8 g) + ½ tsp Cajun Seasoning Mix* (page 183), divided

8 tortillas*

½ cup (120 g) mayonnaise

1 cup (120 g) shredded mozzarella cheese

2 Roma tomatoes, diced

1 cup (70 g) shredded lettuce

1 green onion, thinly sliced

* Use gluten-free tortillas and Cajun Seasoning Mix to make these wraps gluten-free.

In a saucepan, combine the pulled pork, tomato sauce, water and 1 tablespoon (8 g) of the Cajun Seasoning Mix. Cook over medium heat until the pulled pork is heated through.

Moisten the tortillas and heat in the microwave for 30 seconds to 1 minute to make them more flexible.

In a small bowl, combine the mayonnaise and remaining ½ teaspoon Cajun Seasoning Mix. Spread 1 tablespoon (15 g) of the seasoned mayo on each tortilla.

Divide the pulled pork among the tortillas. Top with the cheese, tomatoes, lettuce and onion.

Fold the bottom of the wrap toward the center. Fold one side of the wrap toward the center and keep rolling to close. Repeat until all of the wraps are closed.

PREP-AHEAD TIP: The Cajun-spiced pulled pork can be made ahead of time and stored in the refrigerator for 2 or 3 days or in the freezer for up to 3 months. You can also make the seasoned mayo ahead of time and store in a sealed container in the refrigerator.

RUSTIC PORK AND SWEET POTATO PIE WITH OATMEAL CRUST

BEST BATCH-COOKING METHOD: Any

You are going to have to trust me on this one. I know it sounds like a crazy combination, and it may be, but the ingredients work well together.

If you don't have an oven-safe skillet, you can transfer the pork and sweet potatoes to a greased pie dish before adding the crust.

Crust

1½ cups (120 g) rolled oats* (not quick oats)

¼ cup (56 g) butter

¼ cup (60 ml) water

1 tbsp (15 g) brown sugar

Filling

2 tbsp (28 g) butter

4 green onions, thinly sliced

1 medium apple, cut into bite-size pieces

2 small sweet potatoes, cut into bite-size pieces

1½ cups (355 ml) Vegetable Broth* (page 193)

2 tbsp (16 g) cornstarch

2 tsp (0.5 g) parsley

1 tsp thyme

½ tsp rosemary

¼ tsp sage

2 cups (300 g) diced cooked pork

Use gluten-free oats and Vegetable Broth to make this dish gluten-free.

To make the crust, grind the oats in a blender or food processor until it is a fine flour.

Place the oat flour in a bowl. Cut the butter into the flour. Slowly stir in the water and brown sugar. Mix well, then form into a ball.

Roll out the crust between 2 pieces of parchment or wax paper.

Preheat the oven to 350°F (180°C, or gas mark 4).

To make the filling, add the butter, onion, apple and sweet potatoes to a skillet. Cook over medium heat for 5 minutes.

In a small bowl, whisk together the vegetable broth and cornstarch. Add to the sweet potato mixture. Add the spices and pork to the skillet and cook over medium heat until the sauce thickens.

Remove from the heat. Remove one of the pieces of wax paper from the pie crust. Center the crust over the top of the skillet, then peel off the other piece of wax paper. Use a fork to press the crust into place around the skillet. Cut 3 or 4 small slits in the top of the crust.

Bake for 25 to 30 minutes, or until the pie crust begins to brown.

PREP-AHEAD TIP: You can assemble this dish, cover it and store it in the refrigerator for 1 to 2 days before baking it.

HAM AND SPINACH
WAFFLE QUESADILLAS

What is more fun than a quesadilla? A quesadilla cooked in a waffle maker! I use a pizza cutter to cut the quesadillas into fourths and begin serving them after 2 quesadillas have been made. I continue to replenish our supply of hot quesadillas as they are done cooking in the waffle maker.

While the goal is to sit down and eat dinner together as a family, quesadillas work well for those days when everyone has a different schedule and is eating on the fly.

Oil or spray-on oil

2 cups (240 g) shredded Swiss cheese

16 soft tortillas*

8 thin slices ham

½ cup (75 g) diced red bell pepper

2 cups (140 g) spinach leaves

* Use gluten-free tortillas to make this dish gluten-free.

Preheat the waffle iron. Coat it with oil.

Place 2 tablespoons (16 g) of cheese on a tortilla. Place a slice of ham on top of the cheese. Sprinkle 1 tablespoon (9 g) of red pepper on top of the ham. Spread ¼ cup (18 g) of spinach leaves over the ham. Add 2 more tablespoons (16 g) of cheese over the spinach. Top with another tortilla.

Place the quesadilla on the waffle iron. Close and cook until it is browned, 3 to 4 minutes.

Place on a plate and cover with foil while you repeat the steps and make the rest of the quesadillas.

You can use a pizza cutter to cut the quesadillas into fourths before serving.

PREP-AHEAD TIP: This is already a fast and easy recipe, but you can speed the prep time even more by shredding the cheese and dicing the pepper ahead of time.

THAI PULLED PORK WRAPS

BEST BATCH-COOKING METHOD: Slow Cooker ⌒ Pressure Cooker ⌒ Roasting

Serves: 8

One of the main reasons that I don't cook a whole pork roast with one combination of seasonings is because there are so many flavorful possibilities for serving pulled pork. Why commit 3 or 4 pounds (1365 or 1820 g) of pork to one flavor? By cooking a large pork roast in a slow cooker and pulling it without adding any seasoning initially means I can create five or six different meals, each with a very different combination of spices and seasonings.

¼ cup (68 g) peanut butter

¼ cup (60 ml) water

2 tbsp (30 ml) soy sauce*

2 tbsp (30 ml) lime juice

1 clove garlic, minced

1 tsp grated ginger

1 tsp sesame oil

1 tsp honey or sugar

2 drops hot sauce*

2 cups (300 g) pulled pork

2 cups (330 g) cooked rice

8 large lettuce leaves

* Substitute gluten-free soy sauce and hot sauce to make this recipe gluten-free.

In a small pot, combine the peanut butter, water, soy sauce, lime juice, garlic, ginger, sesame oil, honey and hot sauce.

Cook over medium heat until the peanut sauce is smooth and bubbly.

Add the pulled pork to the peanut sauce in the pot and stir until thoroughly combined. Cook for 2 to 3 minutes, or until the pork is heated through.

Divide the rice among the lettuce leaves. Top the rice with the pulled pork. Roll the lettuce leaves to close.

PREP-AHEAD TIP: The pork can be made in advance and stored in the refrigerator for 2 or 3 days or in the freezer for up to 3 months.

JAMAICAN JERK PORK STUFFED ZUCCHINI

BEST BATCH-COOKING METHOD: Slow Cooker ↷ Pressure Cooker ↷ Roasting

Usually when you make Jamaican jerk, you rub spices into the meat before cooking it. Because this recipe calls for cooked pulled pork, I use the spices that are commonly found in the rub to make a jerk-inspired sauce to coat the pork, rice and peas.

Jerk Sauce

2 tbsp (30 ml) orange juice

1½ tsp (4 g) cornstarch

1 tbsp (15 ml) olive oil

3 tbsp (45 ml) white vinegar*

1 tbsp (15 ml) soy sauce*

2 tsp (10 ml) lime juice

1 tbsp (15 g) brown sugar

½ tsp allspice

½ tsp dried thyme

½ tsp onion powder

½ tsp garlic powder

¼ tsp ground sage

¼ tsp Pumpkin Pie Spice Mix (page 185)

Pinch of cayenne pepper

Stuffed Zucchini

4 small zucchini

1 cup (150 g) pulled pork

1 cup (165 g) cooked rice

¾ cup (93 g) frozen peas, thawed and patted dry

½ cup (60 g) shredded mozzarella cheese

1 medium jalapeño, seeded and thinly sliced

Substitute gluten-free soy sauce and vinegar to make this recipe gluten-free.

Preheat the oven to 350°F (180°C, or gas mark 4). Grease a casserole dish.

To make the sauce, in a small saucepan, use a whisk to combine the orange juice and cornstarch. Add the oil, vinegar, soy sauce, lime juice, sugar and spices. Stir well to combine.

Cook over medium heat until the sauce is thick and bubbly.

To make the stuffed zucchini, cut the zucchini in half lengthwise. Scoop out the seeds.

In a medium bowl, combine the pulled pork, rice, peas and jerk sauce.

Divide the Jamaican jerk mixture among the hollowed-out zucchinis. Top the stuffed zucchinis with the cheese and jalapeño slices. Place the stuffed zucchinis in the greased casserole dish. Bake for 25 minutes.

PREP-AHEAD TIP: You can make the jerk sauce and/or the stuffing ahead of time and store in the refrigerator for 1 or 2 days.

SWEET AND SOUR PORK PIZZA ON A RICE PIZZA CRUST

BEST BATCH-COOKING METHOD: Stove Top ⌇ Broiled

This is a fun twist on traditional sweet and sour pork. You can cook this pizza using a regular pizza crust, but if you have extra cooked rice on hand, you can use it to make a fast and easy pizza crust.

Pizza Crust

3 cups (495 g) cooked rice

1 cup (120 g) shredded mozzarella cheese

2 eggs, beaten

Sweet and Sour Sauce

⅔ cup (160 ml) rice vinegar

2 tbsp (16 g) cornstarch

½ cup (120 g) brown sugar

2 tbsp (30 g) ketchup

2 tsp (10 ml) soy sauce*

3 tbsp (45 ml) water

Topping

1½ cups (275 g) diced cooked pork

½ cup (75 g) red pepper strips

½ cup (80 g) onion strips

½ cup (82 g) pineapple chunks, drained (Save the juice to use in a smoothie!)

1 cup (120 g) shredded mozzarella cheese

* Substitute gluten-free soy sauce to make this recipe gluten-free.

Preheat the oven to 375°F (190°C, or gas mark 5) and grease a pizza pan.

To make the pizza crust, add the rice, mozzarella cheese and beaten eggs to a medium bowl. Stir until thoroughly combined. Form into a circle on the greased pizza pan. Bake for 10 minutes.

While the crust is baking, make the sauce. Whisk together the vinegar and cornstarch in a small pot. Add the sugar, ketchup, soy sauce and water. Cook over medium heat, stirring regularly, until the sauce thickens.

Spread half of the sweet and sour sauce evenly over the pizza crust.

To make the topping, stir the diced pork into the remaining half of the sweet and sour sauce. Spread the pork over the top of the pizza crust. Alternate laying red pepper and onion strips on top of the pork. Sprinkle the pineapple chunks over the top of the pizza. Then sprinkle the cheese over the pizza.

Bake for 12 to 15 minutes, or until the cheese has melted and just begun to brown.

PREP-AHEAD TIP: You can slice the pepper and onion into strips ahead of time and store in a sealed container for 2–3 days in the refrigerator or up to 3 months in the freezer.

Simply Delicious Beef

My parents raised cows, so I was lucky to grow up with an abundance of grass-fed beef that could just be pulled from the freezer. After moving out, I experienced sticker shock the first time I went shopping for beef. Fortunately, I was familiar with the different cuts of beef and was able to find a tender cut that was within my budget.

The price of beef continues to climb. On a recent visit to the grocery store, I was surprised to see ground beef selling for as much per pound as some cuts of steak and more per pound than some of the roasts. Although beef is more expensive than chicken or pork, it is still possible to save money on beef. I check the sales fliers at my local grocery stores, searching for the best deals. When I find a great deal, I stock up and freeze the meat.

When shopping for beef, I recommend being flexible. Look at the different cuts and compare prices. If the tri-tip is expensive, substitute it with sirloin steak. If ground beef is expensive, ask your butcher to grind a sirloin roast for you. Your butcher will often happily package the ground sirloin into usable 1-, 2-, or 3-pound (455-, 910-, or 1365-g) packages for you, which will save you time when you get home if you are planning on freezing your ground beef instead of browning it.

Don't buy convenience cuts like stew meat or fajita meat. You pay a premium for convenience cuts. Instead, buy a chuck roast and cut up your own stew meat. Buy a skirt steak or flank steak and cut it into strips for your fajitas.

You can freeze uncooked ground beef for up to 3 months, roasts for up to 4 months and steaks for up to 6 months. Freezer burn can degrade the quality of your meat, so wrap it well if you repackage it or feel that the store packaging has been compromised. You should not thaw and refreeze raw meat. However, you can thaw ground beef, steaks or roasts, cook them, repackage the cooked meat in airtight containers or freezer bags, and then freeze the cooked meat for up to 3 months.

HOW TO BATCH COOK BEEF IN A SLOW COOKER

The slow cooker is ideal for making shredded beef. I like to use a 3- to 4-pound (1365- to 1820-g) chuck roast. It is an inexpensive cut and the marbling and connective tissue soften during slow cooking, making it easy to shred. You can also use arm roasts and rump roasts.

- » Cut your roast into 3 or 4 large pieces.
- » Place your roast in the slow cooker, add 1 cup (235 ml) of Beef Broth* (page 192) or water, and sprinkle with Seasoned Salt* (page 183) and pepper.
- » Place the lid on the slow cooker and cook on low for 7–8 hours or high for 4 to 6 hours. It should be so tender that it easily shreds with a fork.
- » Place the pieces of meat in a large bowl and while they are still warm, shred with two forks.
- » Use what you need and allow the rest to cool. Then divide the shredded beef into 2-cup (400-g) containers or freezer bags.

*Use gluten-free Beef Broth and Seasoned Salt to make this gluten-free.

HOW TO BATCH BROIL STEAKS

Broiling is a fast and effective way to cook steaks. It seals in the moisture and produces a tender steak. You can do this with just about any inexpensive steak, but I most often use sirloin. The cooking time will vary depending on the thickness of the meat. Very thick steaks can take up to 12 minutes on each side.

- » Preheat the oven's broiler and set the oven rack 6-inches (15-cm) from the heat source.
- » Brush or rub the steak with olive oil and sprinkle it with Seasoned Salt* (page 183) and pepper.
- » Place the steaks on a broiling pan.
- » Broil for 8 to 12 minutes. Then flip and broil for an additional 8 to 12 minutes, or until it is cooked through and the juices run clear.
- » Let the meat rest for 5 minutes, then cut it into cubes or strips.

*Use gluten-free Seasoned Salt to make this gluten-free.

HOW TO BATCH COOK BEEF ON THE STOVE TOP

This is the way I most often prep meat that I plan to use in stir-fries, fajitas and stews. You can use this method to quickly batch cook strips or cubes of beef. The meat cooks quickly, sealing in the juices. I first use a knife to cut a 2- to 3-pound (910- to 1365-g) roast into ½- to 1-inch (1.3- to 2.5-cm) thick "steaks." Then I use kitchen scissors to quickly cut the meat into the desired size pieces.

- » Cut the meat into bite-size pieces or thin strips.
- » Add 1 tablespoon (15 ml) of olive oil to a large heated skillet.
- » Add the pieces of meat to the skillet and cook over medium-high heat until browned on all sides.
- » Lower the heat and cook for 4 to 5 minutes, or until the meat is cooked through and the juices run clear.

Note: If you want to batch cook whole roasts in the oven, follow the directions for Sunday Night Roast Beef on page 87.

HOW TO BATCH COOK BEEF IN A PRESSURE COOKER

You can cook a wide variety of cuts in the pressure cooker. You can use the pressure cooker to quickly produce shredded beef or to make it easy to cut the meat into cubes or strips. I usually cook a chuck roast, round roast or round steaks. Be sure to familiarize yourself with your pressure cooker's manual to ensure you are using it properly.

» Brown the meat in the pressure cooker if you have a stove top pressure cooker or in a large frying pan if you have an electric pressure cooker.

» Remove the meat and place the cooking rack in the bottom of the pressure cooker.

» Add 1 cup (235 ml) of Beef Broth* (page 192), Vegetable Broth* (page 193) or water to the pressure cooker (use 2 cups [470 ml] if your pressure cooker has a removable pressure regulator).

» Set the meat on the rack.

» Cook a 1½- to 2-pound (680- to 910-g) roast for 35 to 40 minutes or a 3-pound (1365-g) roast for 50 to 55 minutes at high pressure. Cook 2 to 3 pounds (910 to 1365 g) of round steak for 15 to 20 minutes at high pressure.

» Use the natural pressure release method to stop the cooking.

*Use gluten-free Beef Broth to make this gluten-free.

HOW TO BATCH COOK GROUND BEEF

I like to batch cook ground beef as soon as I get home from the store. After the ground beef is cooked, I drain off the fat and package it in 1- and 2-cup (225- and 450-g) quantities. Occasionally, I use the ground beef to make meatballs; when I do I make at least 3 pounds (1365 g) at one time. You will find my Baked Meatballs recipe on page 107.

» Place 2 to 3 pounds (910 to 1365 g) of ground beef in a large pot on the stove. Cook it over medium-high heat until it is completely cooked through. You need to turn it regularly to prevent it from burning. You should also use a wood spoon or spatula to break up the meat into small, equal-size pieces.

» If you have a large amount of ground beef, you can batch cook it in a slow cooker. Place 3 to 5 pounds (1365 to 2275 g) of ground beef in the slow cooker. Cook it on high for 2 to 3 hours or on low for 4 to 6 hours. You don't need to watch it as closely as when it is on the stove top, but you do need to occasionally break up the pieces as it cooks to ensure it you have small pieces when it is done cooking.

» Place a colander over a bowl. Spoon the cooked ground beef into the colander and allow it to drain.

» Once the ground beef cools to room temperature, divide it into airtight containers or heavy-duty freezer bags. Cooked ground beef can be stored in the refrigerator for 3 or 4 days or in the freezer for up to 3 months.

STORING THE COOKED BEEF

Place 2 cups (400 g) of cubed or shredded cooked beef in airtight containers or freezer bags. Allow the meat to come to room temperature before placing it in the refrigerator or freezer. Store cooked beef for 3 to 4 days in the refrigerator or up to 3 months in the freezer.

Thaw frozen beef in the refrigerator overnight. If you freeze your meat in a microwave-safe dish, you can quickly thaw it in the microwave. If you are adding the meat to a soup, stew or chili recipe, you can add it frozen and adjust the cooking time.

SOUTHWESTERN SLOPPY JOES

BEST BATCH-COOKING METHOD: Slow Cooker ∾ Stove Top

Serves: 4

For some odd reason, when I was a child I liked the ingredients in tacos, but did not like eating crunchy taco shells. When I could get away with it, I would put taco meat on a hamburger bun instead. I got over my aversion to taco shells a long time ago, but I still enjoy adding taco meat to hamburger buns and making a Southwestern Sloppy Joe.

1 tbsp (15 ml) olive oil

½ cup (80 g) diced onion

⅓ cup (50 g) diced bell pepper

2 cloves garlic, minced

1 cup (245 g) cooked ground beef

1 cup (250 g) cooked pinto beans, kidney beans, or black beans

¾ cup (180 g) tomato sauce

1 tbsp (8 g) Taco Seasoning Mix* (page 184)

4 hamburger buns*

Thin slices of cheddar cheese (optional)

1 cup (70 g) shredded lettuce (optional)

1 medium tomato, thinly sliced (optional)

* Use gluten-free Taco Seasoning Mix and buns to make this gluten-free.

Heat the olive oil in a skillet. Add the onion, bell pepper and garlic. Sauté until the onion is tender, approximately 5 minutes.

Add the ground beef, beans, tomato sauce and taco seasoning. Stir well. Cook over medium heat until the ground beef is heated through.

Serve on hamburger buns, topped with the cheese, lettuce and tomato.

PREP-AHEAD TIP: You can make the Sloppy Joe mixture ahead of time and store it in the refrigerator for 2 or 3 days or in the freezer for up to 3 months.

Serves: 4

BIEROCK SOUP

BEST BATCH-COOKING METHOD: Slow Cooker ∽ Stove Top

Bierocks are a savory pocket pastry filled with meat and cabbage. Although bierocks are one of my favorite foods, they are quite time-consuming to make, so I like to combine the ingredients used for the bierock filling to make a soup that comes together in less than 20 minutes.

1 tbsp (15 ml) olive oil

1 cup (160 g) diced onion

4 cloves garlic, minced

1 stalk celery, thinly sliced

2 cups (450 g) cooked ground beef

4 cups (940 ml) Beef Broth* (page 192)

4 cups (280 g) shredded cabbage

¼ tsp pepper

Pinch of Seasoned Salt* (page 183)

2 cups (100 g) Croutons* (page 190)

* Use gluten-free croutons, Beef Broth and Seasoned Salt to make this dish gluten-free.

Heat the oil in a large soup pot over medium heat. Add the onion, garlic and celery. Sauté for 5 minutes, or until the onion is tender.

Add the ground beef, broth, cabbage, pepper and salt to the pot.

Cook over medium-high heat until it reaches a boil. Lower the heat and simmer for 10 minutes, or until the cabbage has wilted.

Serve with the croutons.

PREP-AHEAD TIP: This soup can be made 2 or 3 days ahead of time and reheated over medium heat on the evening you want to serve it.

SKILLET STROGANOFF

BEST BATCH-COOKING METHOD: Any

Serves: 4

My mother-in-law makes the most delicious Swedish meatballs smothered in a mushroom sauce. The key ingredient in her recipe is the nutmeg that she adds to the meatballs. Although I love her recipe, it is time-consuming to make. So when I am in a hurry I add nutmeg to this easy Skillet Stroganoff to get the same flavor combination for a fraction of the work.

1 tbsp (15 ml) olive oil

1 cup (160 g) diced onion

2 cloves garlic, minced

2 cups (470 ml) Beef Broth* (page 192), divided

1 cup (235 ml) water

8 oz (227 g) uncooked egg noodles*

2 cups (400 g) cubed cooked roast beef

1 cup (70 g) sliced mushrooms

⅔ cup (160 g) sour cream

½ tsp nutmeg

Pinch of salt and pepper

* Use gluten-free Beef Broth and pasta to make this recipe gluten-free.

Add the olive oil to a large skillet. Heat over medium-high heat until hot. Add the onions and garlic and cook for 2 to 3 minutes, until lightly browned.

Add 1¾ cups (410 ml) of the beef broth, water and noodles. Bring to a boil. Reduce the heat, cover and simmer for 6 to 8 minutes, or until the pasta is al dente.

Stir in the beef, mushrooms, sour cream and remaining ¼ cup (60 ml) beef broth. Add the nutmeg, salt and pepper to taste. Cook, stirring constantly, for 3 minutes, or until the beef is heated through.

PREP-AHEAD TIP: You can dice the onions and slice the mushrooms ahead of time if you want to speed the prep time.

BAKED ITALIAN SPRING ROLLS

BEST BATCH-COOKING METHOD: Slow Cooker ❧ Stove Top

Serves: 4–6

I enjoy mixing ingredients from different cuisines to create unique recipes. In this recipe, I have taken Italian seasoned meat and spinach and rolled it in a spring roll wrapper. While spring rolls are often considered an appetizer, these Baked Italian Spring Rolls make a filling dinner.

If you haven't worked with spring roll wrappers before, you will be pleased to discover that they are actually easier to work with than tortillas or pasta. You just submerge them in warm water for 15 seconds and they become very pliable.

---

1 tbsp (15 ml) olive oil

½ cup (80 g) diced onion

¼ cup (38 g) bell pepper

2 cloves garlic, minced

10 oz (280 g) frozen spinach, thawed and drained

1 tbsp (8 g) Italian Seasoning Mix* (page 184)

2 cups (450 g) cooked ground beef

1 cup (120 g) shredded cheddar cheese

1¼ cup (150 g) shredded mozzarella cheese

18 spring roll papers*

2 cups (470 ml) Spaghetti Sauce* (page 188), for dipping

Use gluten-free Italian Seasoning Mix, Spaghetti Sauce and rice papers to make these gluten-free.

Preheat the oven to 425°F (220°C, or gas mark 7). Line a large baking sheet with parchment paper.

Add the olive oil to a large skillet. Add the onion, pepper and garlic and sauté until the onion is tender, approximately 5 minutes.

While the onion is cooking, make sure all the liquid is squeezed out of the thawed spinach.

Add the spinach, Italian seasoning mix and ground beef. Stir until thoroughly combined. Cook over medium heat for 5 minutes. Remove from the heat.

In a small bowl, combine the cheeses.

Fill a casserole dish with warm water. Set a spring roll wrapper in the water for 15 seconds. Remove and place the wrapper on a plate. Place 3 tablespoons (45 g) of the ground beef and spinach mixture in one corner of the wrapper. Sprinkle 2 tablespoons (15 g) cheese over the top. Fold the corner with the filling in it toward the center. Fold each side of the wrapper toward the center. Finish rolling to seal. Place the filled spring roll on the baking sheet.

Repeat until all the wrappers are filled. Bake for 10 minutes. Roll the spring rolls over and bake for an additional 10 minutes. Serve with spaghetti sauce.

PREP-AHEAD TIP: You can make the filling the night before.

SUNDAY NIGHT ROAST BEEF
(HOW TO BATCH COOK ROAST BEEF IN THE OVEN)

Serves: 8–12

This is the method of batch cooking beef that I use the least often. It's not that we don't enjoy it—we do—but it ties up the oven for quite a few hours. However, if there is a special occasion when I want to make a fancy dinner, I use this method to make a tender roast with an inexpensive cut of beef such as a cross rib roast. This also creates lots of leftover meat that can be cubed, sliced or shredded and used in recipes throughout the week.

3½- to 6-lb (1595- to 2730-g) chuck or cross rib roast

2 to 3 tbsp (30 to 45 ml) olive oil

1 tsp garlic powder

1 tsp onion powder

1 tsp smoked paprika

½ tsp Seasoned Salt* (page 183)

¼ tsp pepper

* Use gluten-free Seasoned Salt to make this gluten-free.

Preheat the oven to 500°F (250°C, or gas mark 10).

Place the roast in a roasting pan, brush it with oil, and sprinkle the garlic powder, onion powder, paprika, salt and pepper over the roast. Flip the roast so the fat side is up.

Place it in the oven and roast for 25 minutes. Turn the oven down to 200°F (100°C) and cook for 25 minutes per pound (455 g), or until the internal temperature of the roast is at least 145°F (63°C).

Remove the roast from the oven and let it rest for 20 minutes.

Slice and serve dinner while you allow the rest of the roast to cool off.

Cut the remaining roast into bite-size pieces or strips. Place the cut beef in airtight containers or freezer bags and store it for use in recipes throughout the week.

PHILLY CHEESESTEAK QUESADILLAS

BEST BATCH-COOKING METHOD: Stove Top ∽ Broiled

Serves: 4–6

I often have all the ingredients needed to make Philly cheesesteak sandwiches, except for the bread. I am not a sandwich person, so it rarely occurs to me to pick up sandwich bread when I am at the store. Tortillas, however, are a staple in my kitchen, so I often turn some of my husband's favorite sandwiches into quesadillas.

I have a large electric skillet that I usually use when making quesadillas because I can cook four at one time if I stagger them, but they can be made in smaller batches on the stove top.

1 tbsp (15 ml) olive oil

16 small tortillas*

2 cups (240 g) shredded provolone or Swiss cheese

1 cup (150 g) sliced red or green bell pepper

2 cups (400 g) cooked beef strips

1 cup (160 g) sliced red onion

* Use gluten-free tortillas to make these quesadillas gluten-free.

Brush a pan with oil and heat until hot. (Set an electric skillet to 350°F [180°C] or medium-high on the stove.)

Place as many tortillas on the pan as will fit.

Sprinkle 2 tablespoons (16 g) of cheese on each tortilla. Place the pepper strips on top of the cheese. Place the beef strips over the peppers. Sprinkle the sliced onions over the meat. Top with 2 tablespoons (16 g) of cheese. Place another tortilla on top and press it down to evenly smush the ingredients between the tortillas.

Cook until the bottom tortillas are browned. Flip with a large spatula and cook until the tortillas on the other side are brown, 3 to 4 minutes each side. The tortillas will shrink as they are cooking. After I flip the quesadillas over, I watch to see when the bottom tortilla has shrunk to the same size as the top tortilla to gauge when it is nearly done.

Repeat until all of your quesadillas have been made. You may need to add more oil to the pan between batches.

Cut the quesadillas in half and serve while hot.

PREP-AHEAD TIP: You can slice the onions and peppers 2 or 3 days ahead of time. You can also shred the cheese in advance.

CHILI PIE
WITH SWEET POTATO TOPPING

BEST BATCH-COOKING METHOD: Slow Cooker ⌒ Stove Top

I love pairing sweet potatoes with spicy ingredients. In this recipe, the sweet potatoes help temper the heat of the chili.

Mashed Sweet Potato

2 sweet potatoes, peeled and cut into bite-size pieces

2 tbsp (28 g) butter

1 tsp thyme

1 tsp garlic powder

Chili

1 tbsp (15 ml) olive oil

½ cup (80 g) diced onion

½ cup (75 g) diced bell pepper

2 cloves garlic, minced

1 cup (180 g) diced tomato

1¾ cups (438 g) cooked black beans

1 cup (245 g) cooked ground beef

1 tsp chili powder

½ tsp ground cumin

½ tsp oregano

⅛ tsp ground cayenne pepper

To make the mashed sweet potatoes, pour 2 inches (5 cm) of water into the bottom of a pan. Heat to boiling. Once boiling, add the sweet potato pieces to a steamer basket, place the basket in the pot and steam for 7 minutes.

Preheat the oven to 350°F (180°C, or gas mark 4). Grease an 8 x 8-inch (20 x 20-cm) baking dish.

While the sweet potatoes are steaming, make the chili. Heat the oil in a large skillet. Add the onion, bell pepper and garlic and sauté for 5 minutes, or until the onions are tender.

Add the tomatoes, beans, ground beef, chili powder, cumin, oregano and cayenne pepper. Cook over medium-high heat until it reaches a boil. Lower the heat and simmer for 10 minutes.

While the chili is simmering, continue with the mashed sweet potatoes. Transfer the sweet potatoes to a bowl and mash with a fork. Add the butter, thyme and garlic powder. Then mix with a blender until smooth and creamy.

Transfer the chili to the greased baking dish. Spoon the mashed sweet potatoes over the chili and smooth out to the edges.

Bake for 15 to 20 minutes, or until the sweet potatoes are just beginning to brown.

PREP-AHEAD TIP: You can make the chili ahead of time and store it in the refrigerator for 2 or 3 days. To save even more time, bake the sweet potatoes ahead of time instead of steaming them right before assembling the chili pie.

FAJITA FRITTATA

BEST BATCH-COOKING METHOD: Any

We love fajitas, but we rarely have time to light the barbecue during the week. This quick and easy frittata recipe comes together in less time that it would take to heat the coals.

1 tbsp (15 ml) olive oil

1 cup (160 g) sliced onion

2 cups (300 g) green, red and/or yellow bell peppers, cut into strips, divided

2 cups (400 g) cooked beef strips

8 eggs

2 tsp (6 g) Taco Seasoning Mix*
(page 184)

1 cup (120 g) shredded cheddar cheese, divided

1 cup (120 g) shredded Monterey Jack cheese, divided

* Use gluten-free Taco Seasoning Mix to make this dish gluten-free.

Preheat the oven to broil.

Heat the olive oil in an oven-safe frying pan over medium-high heat. Add the onion and most of the peppers (leave a few pepper strips to add to the top of the frittata before broiling). Cook for 5 minutes, or until the onion is lightly browned and the peppers are tender. Add the beef strips and cook for an additional 2 minutes, or until the meat is heated through.

Add the eggs to a small bowl and beat with a fork or an eggbeater. Add the Taco Seasoning Mix, ¾ cup (90 g) of the cheddar cheese and ¾ cup (90 g) of the Monterey Jack cheese to the eggs and mix well.

Pour the eggs over the meat and peppers. Cook over medium-low heat until the eggs are almost set, 4 to 5 minutes.

Remove the pan from the heat. Arrange the remaining pepper strips on top of the eggs. Sprinkle the remaining ¼ cup (30 g) cheddar cheese and the remaining ¼ cup (30 g) Monterey Jack cheese over the top of the frittata.

Place the frying pan 4 to 6 inches (10 to 15 cm) beneath the broiler. Broil for 2 to 4 minutes, or until the eggs are cooked through and beginning to brown.

PREP-AHEAD TIP: You can speed up prep time by cutting the peppers and onions into strips the day before.

CABBAGE ROLL CASSEROLE

BEST BATCH-COOKING METHOD: Slow Cooker ∽ Stove Top

This deconstructed cabbage roll casserole has all the delicious flavors of traditional cabbage rolls, but without all the work. The layers of cabbage and rice take on the flavor of the Italian seasoning, creating a tasty, if somewhat unconventional, casserole.

1 tbsp (15 ml) olive oil

1 cup (160 g) diced onion

2 stalks celery, thinly sliced

4 cloves garlic, minced

1 cup (130 g) julienned carrot

2 cups (450 g) cooked ground beef

2 cups (330 g) cooked rice

1¾ cups (315 g) diced tomatoes

1¾ cups (430 g) tomato sauce

1 tbsp (8 g) Italian Seasoning Mix*
(page 184)

Pinch of salt and pepper

4 cups (280 g) chopped cabbage

1 cup (120 g) shredded mozzarella
cheese

Use gluten-free Italian Seasoning Mix to make this dish gluten-free.

Preheat the oven to 375°F (190°C, or gas mark 5) and grease a casserole dish.

Heat the oil in a large pot. Add the onion, celery, garlic and carrot. Sauté for 5 minutes, or until the onions are tender.

Add the ground beef, rice, diced tomatoes, tomato sauce, Italian seasoning mix, salt and pepper to the onion mixture. Cook over medium-high heat until it begins to boil. Lower the heat and simmer for 5 minutes.

Layer half of the cabbage in the greased casserole dish. Layer half of the meat and rice mixture over the cabbage. Repeat with the remaining ingredients.

Sprinkle the cheese over the top and bake for 30 minutes, or until the cabbage is wilted and the sauce is bubbly.

PREP-AHEAD TIP: You can prepare the casserole ahead of time and store it in the refrigerator for 2 days or the freezer for up to 3 months.

ASIAN BEEF AND BROCCOLI SLAW WRAPS

BEST BATCH-COOKING METHOD: Stove Top ⌒ Broiled

This is a fun twist on traditional beef and broccoli. If you want to make the wraps even more filling, you can add cooked rice to them.

3 tbsp (45 ml) water

2 tsp (6 g) cornstarch

3 tbsp (45 ml) soy sauce*

1 tbsp (15 ml) rice vinegar

1 tsp sugar

1 tsp grated ginger

3 tbsp (45 g) plain yogurt

1 tsp honey or sugar

1 cup (70 g) matchstick-size broccoli stalks

½ cup (65 g) matchstick-size carrot strips

½ cup (35 g) shredded cabbage

2 tbsp (20 g) diced red bell pepper

2 cups (400 g) cooked beef strips

4 large tortillas or wraps*

1 cup (160 g) cooked rice

Use gluten-free soy sauce and gluten-free tortillas to make this recipe gluten-free.

In a small pot, combine the water, cornstarch, soy sauce, rice vinegar, sugar and ginger. Cook over medium heat until the sauce thickens.

In a medium bowl, combine the yogurt and honey. Add 2 teaspoons (10 ml) of the thickened sauce to the yogurt mixture. Mix well. Add the broccoli, carrots, cabbage and peppers. Stir to coat with the dressing.

Add the beef strips to the remaining sauce in the pot. Stir to coat.

Heat the tortillas in the microwave if necessary to make them more pliable.

Place a large wrap on a plate. If you wish, divide the rice between the tortillas. Spoon one-fourth of the meat mixture onto it just to one side of the center. Top with one-fourth of the broccoli slaw. Fold the top and bottom in toward the center of the wrap. Fold the side closest to the beef and broccoli toward the middle and then keep rolling until the wrap is closed.

Repeat until all of the wraps are made.

PREP-AHEAD TIP: You can make the Asian Beef and the Broccoli Slaw the day before and store them in a salad container in the refrigerator. Reheat the beef before adding it to the wrap.

FRENCH DIP PIZZA ON FRENCH BREAD

BEST BATCH-COOKING METHOD: Slow Cooker ∾ Pressure Cooker ∾ Roasting

You can make this on a traditional pizza crust, but my family enjoys it when I make these "pizzas" on French bread, which speeds up the prep time. As soon as the onions are caramelized, I can pile everything on top of the French bread and pop them in the oven.

Pizza

1 tbsp (15 ml) olive oil

1 tbsp (15 ml) balsamic vinegar

¼ cup (60 ml) beef consommé*

2 red onions, thinly sliced

1 loaf French bread*, cut in half horizontally

2 cups (400 g) shredded beef

2 cups (240 g) shredded Swiss cheese

Horseradish Sauce

1 tbsp (14 g) butter

1 tbsp (8 g) cornstarch

Pinch of Seasoned Salt* (page 183) and pepper

1 cup (235 ml) milk

1 tbsp (15 g) horseradish

1 tsp garlic powder

Use gluten-free beef consommé or Beef Broth (page 192), gluten-free Seasoned Salt and gluten-free French bread or baguettes to make this recipe gluten-free.

To make the pizzas, add the olive oil, vinegar and beef consommé to a skillet. Add the sliced onions and cook over medium heat for 10 minutes, or until they are a deep brown and very tender.

While the onions are sautéing, make the horseradish sauce. Melt the butter in a small saucepot. Stir in the cornstarch, salt and pepper. Cook over low heat until the mixture is smooth and bubbly. Slowly stir in the milk. Heat to boiling, stirring constantly. Lower the heat and stir in the horseradish and garlic powder. Cook for 1 minute.

Preheat the oven to 350°F (180°C, or gas mark 4).

Place the 2 half loaves of bread on a baking sheet with the cut side up. Spread the horseradish sauce over the loaves of bread. Layer the shredded beef over the sauce. Top with the onions and cheese.

Bake for 10 minutes, or until the cheese begins to brown.

Slice and serve while hot.

PREP-AHEAD TIP: If you want to further speed prep time, you can slice the onions into thin rings the night before and store them in an airtight container.

Serves: 4

BARBECUE BEEF PASTA SKILLET

BEST BATCH-COOKING METHOD: Slow Cooker ✑ Pressure Cooker ✑ Roasting

This easy dinner is a hit with my boys! The noodles are cooked in the skillet and then the shredded beef and barbecue sauce are added to the noodles, so you only have one pan to wash. At the very end of the cooking process, I put the dish under the broiler to quickly melt the cheese. This step is optional because the cheese will begin to melt as it sits on top of the hot noodles.

2 cups (470 ml) Vegetable Broth* (page 193), divided

1 cup (235 ml) water

8 oz (227 g) rotini pasta*

2 cups (400 g) cooked shredded beef

1 cup (240 ml) Barbecue Sauce* (page 189)

½ cup (60 g) shredded cheddar cheese

1 green onion, thinly sliced

* Use gluten-free pasta, gluten-free Barbecue Sauce and gluten-free Vegetable Broth to make this dish gluten-free.

Add 1¾ cups (410 ml) of the broth, the water and the pasta to an oven-safe pan. Cook over high heat until it reaches a boil. Lower the heat, cover with a lid and simmer for 8 minutes, or until most of the liquid has been absorbed and the pasta is al dente.

Preheat the broiler.

Add the shredded beef, barbecue sauce and remaining ¼ cup (60 ml) broth to the pan. Stir until the barbecue sauce is thoroughly combined with the other ingredients.

Cook over medium heat for 3 to 4 minutes, or until the shredded beef is heated through.

Top with the cheese and sliced onions.

Place the pan 4 to 6 inches (10 to 15 cm) below the broiler. Broil for 2 to 3 minutes, or until the cheese is melted and begins to brown.

PREP-AHEAD TIP: Make the Barbecue Sauce (page 189) ahead of time. It can be stored in the refrigerator for 4 or 5 days.

COTTAGE PIE WITH CORNBREAD CRUST

Serves: 6

BEST BATCH-COOKING METHOD: Any

Cottage pie is one of my childhood favorites. It is usually topped with mashed potatoes, but when I don't have leftover mashed potatoes, I find it is faster to whip up some cornbread batter than to make a batch of mashed potatoes.

Cottage Pie Ingredients

2 tbsp (30 ml) olive oil

1 cup (160 g) diced onion

3 cloves garlic, minced

1 cup (235 ml) Beef Broth* (page 192)

2 tbsp (16 g) cornstarch

½ cup (120 g) tomato sauce

1 tbsp (15 ml) Worcestershire sauce*

1 potato, diced

1 carrot, diced

1 cup (130 g) frozen corn

1 cup (130 g) frozen peas

2 cups (400 g) diced cooked beef roast

Cornbread Ingredients

¾ cup (105 g) cornmeal

1¼ cups (150 g) flour*

¼ cup (50 g) sugar

2 tsp (6 g) baking powder

½ tsp salt

1 cup (235 ml) milk

1 egg, beaten

2 tbsp (30 ml) oil

* To make the cornbread gluten-free, substitute ½ cup (60 g) rice flour, ½ cup (60 g) tapioca flour, ¼ cup (30 g) potato starch, and 1 teaspoon xanthan gum for the flour.

* Also use gluten-free Beef Broth and Worcestershire sauce to make this pie gluten-free.

Preheat the oven to 400°F (200°C, or gas mark 6).

To make the cottage pie, add the oil to a large oven-safe skillet. Add the onion and sauté for 4 minutes over medium-high heat. Add the garlic to the skillet and cook for 1 minute more.

In a small bowl, whisk together the broth and cornstarch. Add it to the skillet. Add the tomato sauce and Worcestershire sauce to the skillet. Stir to combine all the ingredients.

Add the potatoes and carrots to the skillet. Cook over medium to medium-high heat for 5 minutes.

Add the corn, peas and beef to the skillet. Simmer for 5 minutes.

While the filling is simmering, begin making the cornbread. In a medium bowl, blend together the cornmeal, flour, sugar, baking powder and salt. Add the milk, egg and oil to the dry ingredients; stir just long enough to ensure the dry ingredients are moist.

Remove the skillet from the stove. Pour the cornbread batter on top of the cottage pie filling. Bake for 30 minutes, or until the top begins to brown and an inserted toothpick comes out clean.

PREP-AHEAD TIP: You can make the filling ahead of time and refrigerate it for 1 or 2 days. Then all you need to do is whip up your cornbread batter on the day you want to cook the cottage pie and pour it over the filling before baking.

DUTCH OVEN BORSCHT PASTA BAKE

BEST BATCH-COOKING METHOD: Any

When my kids were little, I discovered that if I soaked up most of the moisture in soups with pasta there were a lot fewer messes on soup night. Now that my kids are older, I rarely turn soups into pasta bakes. However, I do still use this trick with borscht because the beet-red broth, while delicious, does stain.

1 tbsp (15 ml) olive oil

1 tbsp (15 ml) balsamic vinegar

1 cup (160 g) diced onion

4 cloves garlic, minced

2 medium beets, diced

2 medium red potatoes, diced

1 large carrot, cut into thick slices

2 stalks celery, thinly sliced

1¾ cups (315 g) diced tomatoes

1½ cups (300 g) cubed cooked beef

1¾ cups (410 ml) Beef Broth* (page 192)

8 oz (227 g) rotini pasta*

1 bay leaf

Pinch of Seasoned Salt* (page 183) and pepper

Use gluten-free pasta, Beef Broth and Seasoned Salt to make this dish gluten-free.

Preheat the oven to 425°F (220°C, or gas mark 7).

Add the olive oil, balsamic vinegar, onion, garlic, beets, potatoes, carrot and celery to a large oven-safe lidded pot or Dutch oven. Cook over medium heat for 8 minutes.

Add the tomatoes, meat, broth, pasta, bay leaf, salt and pepper. Stir to combine. Put the lid on the pot and cook for 35 minutes, or until the vegetables are tender and the pasta has absorbed most of the liquid.

Remove the bay leaf before serving.

PREP-AHEAD TIP: You can save time by prepping the vegetables the night before. Store the cut potatoes in a bowl of water to prevent them from turning brown.

SWISS STEAK STEW

BEST BATCH-COOKING METHOD: Any

I have always enjoyed the savory tomato sauce that Swiss steak is cooked in. My mom made it in the pressure cooker, so her recipe came together pretty quickly, but I have found that I can combine the same flavors in even less time by making a Swiss steak stew.

---

1 tbsp (15 ml) olive oil

1 cup (160 g) diced onion

1 stalk celery, thinly sliced

3 cloves garlic, minced

2 cups (260 g) thinly sliced carrot

2 medium potatoes, diced

4 cups (940 ml) Beef Broth* (page 192)

¾ cup (180 g) tomato sauce

1 tbsp (8 g) Italian Seasoning Mix* (page 184)

1 bay leaf

Pinch of Seasoned Salt* (page 183) and pepper

¼ cup (60 ml) water

2 tbsp (16 g) cornstarch

2 cups (400 g) cooked cube beef

Use gluten-free Beef Broth, Italian Seasoning Mix and Seasoned Salt to make this stew gluten-free.

Heat the oil in a large soup pot. Add the onion and celery and sauté for 4 minutes. Add the garlic and sauté for 1 minute.

Add the carrot and potatoes to the pot. Continuing cooking over medium-high heat for 5 minutes.

Add the broth, tomato sauce and spices.

In a small bowl, whisk together the water and cornstarch. Add it to the soup pot and mix the ingredients well.

Bring the stew a boil. Reduce the heat and simmer for 10 minutes.

Add the cubed beef and cook for an additional 5 minutes, until heated through.

PREP-AHEAD TIP: This stew can be made in advance and stored in the refrigerator for 2 or 3 days. Reheat over medium-low heat.

SKILLET BEEF BURGUNDY

BEST BATCH-COOKING METHOD: Stove Top

Serves: 4

While I enjoy beef burgundy, most nights I don't have several hours to wait for the wine and broth to be reduced. I speed the process by using beef consommé, which is richer and thicker than broth. I also use much less wine, because it is not afforded as much time to cook off.

This dish is very forgiving. If someone is running late, you can allow it to simmer over low heat without worry about ruining it. If the sauce becomes too thick, just add a little consommé or broth to thin it and continue simmering.

---

2 slices cooked bacon (page 47), crumbled

½ cup (80 g) diced red onion

1 tbsp (15 ml) olive oil

1¼ cups (295 ml) beef consommé*

½ cup (120 ml) red wine

1 bay leaf

1 tsp thyme

2 cups (400 g) cubed cooked beef

12-oz (340-g) package egg noodles*

3 cups (210 g) sliced mushrooms

* Use gluten-free beef consommé or Beef Broth (page 192) to make this dish gluten-free. Serve over gluten-free egg noodles, rice or mashed potatoes to make this recipe gluten-free.

If you don't have cooked bacon on hand, start by cooking 2 slices of bacon. When the bacon is almost done cooking, add the onion and cook the onion until it is tender, approximately 5 minutes. However, if you have cooked bacon on hand, start by sautéing the onion in olive oil. When the onion is tender, crumble the bacon slices, and add it to the onion.

Add the beef consommé, red wine, bay leaf, thyme and beef to the onion. Bring it to a gentle boil, then lower the heat and simmer for 10 minutes.

While the beef burgundy is simmering, cook the egg noodles according to the package directions.

Add the mushrooms to the skillet and simmer for 5 minutes.

Drain the egg noodles. Serve the beef burgundy over the egg noodles.

NOTE: When you have leftover wine, freeze it in usable quantities in a sealable freezer bag or other airtight container. Because wine contains alcohol it does not freeze as hard as water and remains liquid around the edges, so ensure the container is tightly sealed so it doesn't leak. You can add frozen wine directly to recipes and it will naturally thaw quickly.

PREP-AHEAD TIP: You can dice the onions in advance and store in a sealed container for 2 or 3 days in the refrigerator or freeze for up to 3 months. You can slice the mushrooms 1 or 2 days in advance. Place the sliced mushrooms in a bowl and cover with plastic wrap. You can also cook the bacon in advance using the tip for Batch Cooking Bacon in the Oven (see page 47).

ENCHILADA CASSEROLE

BEST BATCH-COOKING METHOD: Slow Cooker ∽ Pressure Cooker ∽ Roasting

This casserole is a lot less messy to make than traditional enchiladas, but it does take longer to bake.

1 tbsp (15 ml) olive oil

1 cup (160 g) diced onion

½ cup (75 g) diced bell pepper

1 cup (200 g) shredded beef

1¾ cups (438 g) cooked black beans

1 cup (130 g) frozen corn, thawed

1½ cups (355 ml) Enchilada Sauce* (page 188), divided

4 cups (660 g) cooked rice

2 eggs, beaten

10 to 12 corn tortillas*

1 cup (120 g) shredded cheddar cheese

1 cup (120 g) shredded mozzarella cheese

Use gluten-free tortillas and Enchilada Sauce to make this recipe gluten-free.

Preheat the oven to 375°F (190°C, or gas mark 5) and grease a 9 x 13-inch (23 x 33-cm) casserole dish.

Add the olive oil, onion and bell pepper to a skillet. Sauté for 5 minutes. Add the shredded beef, beans, corn and ½ cup (120 ml) of the enchilada sauce. Stir to thoroughly combine the ingredients.

In a medium bowl, combine the rice, remaining 1 cup (235 ml) enchilada sauce and eggs.

Cut the tortillas into fourths with a pizza cutter or scissors and layer half of them on the bottom of the casserole dish.

Spread half of the rice mixture over the tortillas. Layer half of the meat mixture over the rice. Sprinkle half of each cheese over the meat mixture. Repeat the layers with the remaining ingredients.

Cover with foil and bake for 30 minutes. Remove the foil and bake for an additional 5 to 10 minutes, or until the cheese is brown and bubbly.

PREP-AHEAD TIP: You can assemble this casserole ahead of time and store it in the refrigerator for 1 day or in the freezer for up to 3 months.

BAKED MEATBALLS
(BATCH COOKING MEATBALLS)

Makes: 65+

I have already admitted that I am not crazy about making meatballs, but that doesn't mean that my family and I don't enjoy eating them. When I do make meatballs, I make a huge batch that will provide enough for several meals and freeze them in usable portions.

I have found it is much easier to make large batches of meatballs if I bake them. Baking also allows me to cook 3 pounds (1365 g) of meatballs in the time that it takes to cook 1 pound (455 g) on the stove top. You also don't have to worry about turning them to make sure they are evenly cooked. To easily make the meatballs all the same size, I use a tablespoon (15 g) size cookie dough scoop to form the balls.

3 lb (1365 g) ground beef

3 tbsp (24 g) cornstarch

2¼ cups (360 g) diced onion

3 eggs

¾ cup (180 ml) Beef Broth* (page 192)

2 tsp (6 g) garlic powder

1½ tsp (5 g) Seasoned Salt* (page 183)

¾ tsp coarsely ground pepper

* Use gluten-free Beef Broth and Seasoned Salt to make the meatballs gluten-free.

Preheat the oven to 400°F (200°C, or gas mark 6) and either grease 2 large baking sheets or line them with foil.

Place the ground beef in a large bowl. Add the cornstarch and mix it into the meat.

Add the onion, eggs, broth and spices. Mix well to fully incorporate all of the ingredients into the meat mixture.

Form 1-inch (2.5-cm) balls and place them on the baking sheets. You can place them fairly close together because they will shrink during cooking.

Place the baking sheets in the oven and bake for 20 minutes.

Remove the meatballs and allow them to cool before packaging. I divide them among three freezer bags. I place one bag in the refrigerator to use within a day or two and freeze the rest for up to 3 months.

MONGOLIAN BEEF MEATBALLS

BEST BATCH-COOKING METHOD: Baked

Warning: These meatballs are addictive. Mongolian beef sauce is similar to the sauce used to make Asian Beef and Broccoli Slaw Wraps (page 95), but it is a little sweeter. This sweet soy sauce glaze has a little kick to it that keeps my family coming back for more. I could eat them for breakfast, lunch and dinner. And on the few occasions when I have had leftovers, I have.

1 tbsp (15 ml) olive oil

2 cloves garlic, minced

¼ cup (60 ml) soy sauce*

¼ cup (60 ml) water

2 tsp (6 g) cornstarch

⅓ cup + 1 tbsp (90 g) brown sugar

1 tsp grated ginger

½ tsp crushed red pepper flakes

20 cooked meatballs (page 107)

1 tbsp (8 g) sesame seeds

1 green onion, thinly sliced

2 cups (330 g) cooked rice

Use gluten-free soy sauce and gluten-free meatballs to make this dish gluten-free.

Heat the oil in a large frying pan or skillet. Add the garlic and cook for 1 minute over medium heat.

In a small bowl, whisk together the soy sauce, water and cornstarch. Add the soy mixture to the skillet.

Add the brown sugar, ginger and red pepper flakes to the skillet. Mix well to combine the ingredients. Cook over medium-low heat until the sauce is thick and bubbly.

Add the meatballs to the skillet. Toss to coat with the sauce. Cook over medium heat for 5 minutes, or until the meatballs are heated through.

Sprinkle the sesame seeds and green onion over the meatballs.

Serve the meatballs over rice.

NOTE: Save money on sesame seeds by purchasing them from the bulk food section instead of the spice aisle. You can usually buy a pound (455 g) of sesame seeds from the bulk bin for less than the price of a 2-ounce (56-g) jar.

CHEATER SWEDISH MEATBALLS

BEST BATCH-COOKING METHOD: Baked

Serves: 4

I absolutely love my mother-in-law's Swedish meatballs. She includes nutmeg in them, which is the equivalent of adding a pinch of awesome. Because I make large batches of plain meatballs, I add nutmeg and allspice to the sauce to capture that flavor without having to make special meatballs just for this dish.

2 tbsp (28 g) butter

1 lb (455 g) fresh mushrooms, sliced

½ cup (80 g) chopped onion

2 cloves garlic, minced

2 tbsp (16 g) cornstarch

½ cup (120 ml) milk, divided

½ cup (120 ml) Vegetable Broth* (page 193)

¼ tsp nutmeg

¼ tsp allspice

20 cooked meatballs* (page 107)

2 cups (330 g) cooked rice

* Use gluten-free Vegetable Broth and meatballs to make this recipe gluten-free.

In a large skillet, melt the butter. Add the mushrooms, onion and garlic. Cook over medium heat, stirring occasionally, until tender, approximately 5 minutes.

In a small bowl, combine the cornstarch and ¼ cup (60 ml) of the milk. Whisk until the mixture is smooth.

Add the cornstarch mixture to the mushroom mixture. Stir well. Slowly add the remaining ¼ cup (60 ml) milk and the broth while stirring continuously.

Add the nutmeg and allspice to the mushroom sauce. Stir well to incorporate the spices.

Add the meatballs to the sauce. Stir continuously while cooking over medium heat. Cook until the mushroom sauce is thick and bubbly and the meatballs are heated through.

Serve over rice.

PREP-AHEAD TIP: If you wish, you can make the mushroom sauce ahead of time and store it in the refrigerator for 1 or 2 days. Reheat it over low heat before adding the meatballs.

APRICOT-GLAZED MEATBALLS

BEST BATCH-COOKING METHOD: Baked

Sweet glazed meatballs are often served as appetizers, but the addition of soy sauce, ginger and red pepper to this glaze lends a touch of savory, which makes them more appropriate for dinner.

½ cup (120 ml) orange juice

2 tsp (6 g) cornstarch

¼ cup (60 g) apricot fruit spread, preserves or jam

2 tbsp (30 ml) soy sauce*

2 tbsp (30 g) brown sugar

1 tsp grated ginger

¼ cup (38 g) diced red bell pepper

20 cooked meatballs* (page 107)

2 cups (330 g) cooked rice

Use gluten-free soy sauce and meatballs to make this dish gluten-free.

In a large skillet or frying pan, whisk together the orange juice and cornstarch. Add the apricot fruit spread, soy sauce, brown sugar, ginger and diced red pepper.

Cook the sauce over medium heat while stirring until thick and bubbly, 2 to 3 minutes.

Add the meatballs to the glaze. Toss to coat the meatballs with the glaze.

Cook the meatballs over medium heat for 5 minutes, or until heated through.

Serve over rice.

PREP-AHEAD TIP: You can make these meatballs in advance and store them in a sealed container in the refrigerator for 2 or 3 days. Reheat in a skillet over low heat.

Fast, Filling Beans and Rice

Beans and rice are frugal additions to meals. Considering the cost of packaged foods, it makes sense to buy dried beans and rice in bulk and cook them from scratch. Canned beans are usually only offered in a few common varieties at the store; there is usually much more variety in the dried beans section.

Both beans and rice freeze well, so they are great ingredients to cook in bulk. Not only will you save money by cooking them from scratch, but you will also save quite a bit of time by having precooked rice on hand. I never cook less than a pound (455 g) of rice or beans when I need to cook some. No matter what variety I am cooking, I know my family can consume that amount in a reasonable period of time. Our favorite rice to eat plain is basmati, so I will often cook up to 4 cups (720 g) of basmati rice at a time, which produces about 10 cups (1650 g) of cooked rice. We consume a lot of black beans, pinto beans and cannellini beans, so I usually cook those beans in 2-pound (910-g) batches, which produces a little over 10 cups (2500 g) of cooked beans per batch.

While rice and beans make great side dishes, I often use them to create frugal, meatless meals. You will find that many of the recipes in this chapter can do double duty and serve as either a side dish or a main course.

PREPARING BEANS

Most cooking methods require that beans be soaked for between 6 and 12 hours.

- » Sort the beans, removing any shriveled or damaged beans. Rinse the beans well.
- » Place beans in a large bowl or pot. Add enough water that the beans are covered by at least 2 inches (5 cm). Soak for 8 hours to overnight.
- » Drain and rinse the beans. Then follow one of the cooking methods below.

HOW TO SPEED SOAK BEANS

You can use this method in place of soaking beans overnight.

- » Add rinsed beans to a large pot and cover with water.
- » Place the pot over high heat and bring to a boil.
- » Remove from the heat, place a lid on the pot and let sit for 1 hour.
- » Drain and rinse the beans. Proceed with one of the cooking methods below.

Note: When you are working with dried kidney beans, you need to boil them for 10 minutes before cooking them on the stove top or slow cooker. This neutralizes a toxin called phytohemagglutinin, which can cause acute digestive distress. You do not need to boil kidney beans if you are cooking them in a pressure cooker.

HOW TO BATCH COOK BEANS ON THE STOVE TOP

The cooking time for beans can vary greatly depending on the age of the beans. Start checking them at 40 minutes and then check every 10 minutes until they reach the desired texture.

- » Sort and rinse the beans. Soak the beans using one of the methods above.
- » Place the beans in a large pot, add 1 teaspoon of salt, and cover with 1 inch (2.5 cm) of cold water.
- » Bring to a boil, then lower the heat and gently simmer for 45 to 90 minutes* or until they are tender.
- » Use the beans in a recipe or allow them to come to room temperature and then store them.

* Chickpeas take 1 to 2 hours to cook on the stove top.

HOW TO BATCH COOK BEANS IN A SLOW COOKER

As with many other foods, batch cooking beans in the slow cooker is the most forgiving method. Start checking your beans for doneness after 5½ hours if cooking on low and 3½ hours if cooking on high and then check every 30 minutes until they reach the desired tenderness.

If I am only cooking 1 pound (455 g) of beans, I use my 3½-quart (3.2-l) slow cooker. When I want to cook 2 pounds (910 g) or more of dried beans, I use my 6-quart (5.4-l) slow cooker.

- » Sort and rinse the beans. Soak the beans using one of the methods above.
- » Place the beans in the slow cooker, add 1 teaspoon of salt and cover with 2 inches (5 cm) of water.
- » Cook on low for 6 to 8 hours or on high for 4 to 5 hours.
- » Once they reach the desired tenderness, use them in a recipe or cool before storing for future use.

HOW TO BATCH COOK BEANS IN A PRESSURE COOKER

Cooking beans in a pressure cooker is the fastest method because you do not have to soak the dried beans before cooking them. In fact, you can cook them from start to finish in less time than it takes to do the quick soak method. For fresh beans, use the shorter cooking time; for older beans, cook longer. Remember, it is always better to have undercooked beans than overcooked mushy beans. You can always cook firm beans a little longer.

Be sure to consult the owner's manual for proper use of your pressure cooker.

» Sort and rinse the beans.

» Add 1 pound (455 g) of beans, 8 cups (1880 ml) of water, 1 teaspoon of salt and 2 tablespoons (30 ml) of olive oil to the pressure cooker.

» Bring to high pressure and cook for the times listed below:

  » Cook black beans for 20 to 25 minutes.

  » Cook red beans for 14 to 20 minutes.

  » Cook pinto beans for 22 to 25 minutes.

  » Cook cannellini beans for 25 to 30 minutes.

  » Cook chickpeas for 30 to 40 minutes.

  » Cook navy beans for 18 to 20 minutes.

» When cooking time is up, use the quick pressure release method to release the pressure.

» After all the steam has been released, check the beans. If they are the desired tenderness, use them in a recipe or allow them to cool before storing them. If they are still too firm, allow them to simmer until they reach the desired tenderness.

HOW TO BATCH COOK LENTILS ON THE STOVE TOP

Lentils do not require soaking prior to cooking. Cooking time varies depending on the type of lentil.

» Sort and rinse the lentils.

» Add 1 pound (455 g) of lentils and 8 cups (1880 ml) of hot water to a large pot.

» Bring the water to a boil, then lower the heat and gently simmer, uncovered, for the times listed below:

  » Cook brown lentils for 30 to 45 minutes.

  » Cook French green, black beluga and yellow lentils for 25 to 30 minutes.

  » Cook unhulled red lentils for 20 to 25 minutes.

  » Cook split red, orange or yellow lentils for 10 minutes.

» Place the cooked lentils in a fine-mesh colander and drain well before using or storing.

» Cooked lentils can be stored in the refrigerator in a sealed container for 3 to 5 days or frozen for up to 3 months.

HOW TO BATCH COOK LENTILS IN A SLOW COOKER

Place 1 pound (455 g) of sorted and rinsed lentils in the slow cooker and cover with water. Cook on low for 4 to 5 hours.

HOW TO BATCH COOK LENTILS IN THE PRESSURE COOKER

» Place 1 pound (455 g) of sorted and rinsed lentils in the pressure cooker. Add 8 cups (1880 ml) of water. Cook at high pressure for the following times:

  » Cook brown lentils in the pressure cooker for 10 to 12 minutes.

  » Cook French green, black beluga and yellow lentils for 8 to 10 minutes.

» Use the quick release method to release pressure.

» I don't recommend cooking red lentils or split lentils in a pressure cooker because they cook so quickly it is easy to overcook them.

HOW TO STORE COOKED BEANS

You can store cooked beans for 3 to 5 days in the refrigerator or up to 6 months in the freezer. I like to place approximately 1¾ cups (438 g) of beans with some of the cooking liquid in an airtight container or freezer bag because that is close to the amount in a can of beans and makes it easy to substitute cooked beans for a can of beans in recipes.

Thaw frozen beans overnight in the refrigerator. If you have stored them in a microwave-safe container, you can thaw them in the microwave.

HOW TO PREPARE RICE

You don't need to sort rice grains, like you do beans. However, I recommend measuring your rice into a fine-mesh strainer and rinsing before cooking. Keep in mind, you shouldn't rinse enriched white rice since that will wash away the nutrients coated on the outside.

Each cup (195 g) of uncooked rice will yield approximately 3 cups (495 g) of cooked rice.

HOW TO BATCH COOK RICE ON THE STOVE TOP

» Place rinsed rice in a large pot. If cooking white rice, add 1½ cups (355 ml) of water for each cup (195 g) of rice. If cooking brown rice, add 1¾ cups (410 ml) of water for each cup (195 g) of rice.

» Bring to a boil. Reduce the heat, cover and simmer on low for 20 minutes for white rice and 50 minutes for brown rice.

» Let stand for 10 minutes. Fluff with a fork.

HOW TO BATCH COOK RICE IN A SLOW COOKER

» Rub the inside of the slow cooker with butter or oil.

» Place the rinsed rice in the slow cooker. If cooking white rice, add 1½ cups (355 ml) of water for each cup (195 g) of rice. If cooking brown rice, add 1¾ cups (410 ml) of water for each cup (195 g) of rice.

» Cook on high for 1½ to 2 hours for white rice and 2¼ to 3 hours for brown rice.

» Fluff with a fork and serve or store for later use.

HOW TO BATCH COOK RICE IN A PRESSURE COOKER

Be sure to consult the owner's manual for proper use of your pressure cooker.

- » Place rinsed rice in a pressure cooker. Use the below ratios of rice to water:
    - » For 2 cups (390 g) of white rice add 3 cups (705 ml) of water. For 3 cups (585 g) of white rice add 4¼ cups (1 L) of water. For 4 cups (780 g) of white rice add 5 cups (1175 ml) of water.
    - » For 2 cups (390 g) of brown rice add 3½ cups (880 ml) of water. For 3 cups (585 g) of brown rice add 5 cups (1175 ml) of water. For 4 cups (780 g) of brown rice add 6½ cups (1530 ml) of water.
- » Add 2 tablespoons (28 g) of butter or (30 ml) oil.
- » Cook white rice at high pressure for 3 minutes, then let the pressure release naturally for 7 minutes. Quick release any remaining pressure. Cook brown rice at high pressure for 10 minutes, then let the pressure release naturally for 10 minutes. Quick release any remaining pressure.

HOW TO BATCH COOK RICE IN THE OVEN

This is my least used batch-cooking method. Why? Because it saves neither time nor energy. However, I will use it if I am already heating up the oven to cook something else. I cook a minimum of 2 cups (390 g) of rice when I bake it in the oven. I usually bake 3 cups (585 g) of rice at a time.

- » Preheat the oven to 400°F (200°C, or gas mark 6). Grease or butter a 9 x 13-inch (23 x 33-cm) baking dish.
- » Place the rice in the baking dish. For every cup (195 g) of white rice add 1½ cups (355 ml) of hot water. For every cup (195 g) of brown rice add 2 cups (470 ml) of hot water.
- » Cover the baking dish tightly with foil.
- » Place in the oven and bake the white rice for 25 minutes and the brown rice for 1 hour.
- » Fluff with a fork.

HOW TO STORE COOKED RICE

Refrigerate rice within 2 hours of cooking it. Store cooked rice in airtight containers or freezer bags. Cooked rice will keep in the refrigerator for 3 to 5 days and in the freezer for up to 6 months. I usually store my cooked rice in 1-, 2- and 4-cup (165-, 330-, and 660-g) quantities, so I have the right size for different recipes.

Thaw frozen rice overnight in the refrigerator. If you have stored it in a microwave-safe container, you can thaw rice in the microwave. You can also add frozen rice directly to soups and it will quickly thaw in the heated liquid.

REHEATING COOKED RICE

You can reheat cooked rice in the microwave, on the stove top or in the oven.

To reheat cooked rice in the microwave, put it in a microwave-safe bowl, sprinkle it with 1 to 2 teaspoons (5 to 10 ml) of water, cover with a damp paper towel and microwave on high for 2 minutes. Then fluff with a fork and check to see if it is heated through. Keep heating it in 1- to 2-minute increments until it is heated through. Fluff with a fork and use as desired.

To reheat cooked rice on the stove, put it in a saucepan with 1 tablespoon (15 ml) of water. Cover and cook over low heat, stirring occasionally, until it is heated through. Fluff with a fork and use as desired.

To reheat cooked rice in the oven, preheat the oven to 400°F (200°C, or gas mark 6). Place the rice in an oven-safe container with 1 tablespoon (15 ml) of water. Cover tightly with foil and bake for 10 minutes or until the rice is heated through.

THREE-BEAN MINESTRONE SOUP

BEST BATCH-COOKING METHOD: Any

The combination of Italian herbs in this soup create a flavorful broth, while the three different beans provide lots of protein, creating a hearty soup that will leave you feeling satisfied with this meatless recipe.

1 tbsp (15 ml) olive oil

½ cup (80 g) minced onion

1 stalk celery, thinly sliced

2 cloves garlic, minced

½ cup (50 g) chopped green beans

⅓ cup (43 g) julienned or shredded carrot

4 cups (940 ml) Vegetable Broth* (page 193)

2 cups (360 g) or 1 (14.5-oz [406-g]) can diced tomatoes

1¾ cups (438 g) cooked black beans

1¾ cups (438 g) cooked white beans

1¾ cups (438 g) cooked garbanzo beans

1 tsp oregano

½ tsp basil

½ tsp thyme

2 cups (140 g) fresh spinach

Use gluten-free Vegetable Broth to make this soup gluten-free.

Heat the olive oil over medium heat in a large pot. Add the onion, celery, garlic, green beans and carrot and sauté for 5 minutes.

Add the vegetable broth, tomatoes, beans and spices to the soup. Stir to combine. Bring the soup to a boil, then reduce the heat and simmer for 10 minutes.

Add the spinach leaves and cook for 5 minutes longer, or until the spinach is wilted.

PREP-AHEAD TIP: This soup can be made in advance and stored in the refrigerator for 2 or 3 days. It also freezes well and can be kept in the freezer for up to 3 months.

BLACK BEAN AND MUSHROOM ENCHILADAS

BEST BATCH-COOKING METHOD: Any

These hearty enchiladas are a delicious alternative to traditional enchiladas. While pound for pound, mushrooms are often more expensive than ground beef, cup for cup, they cost much less. Mushrooms take on the flavors of the other ingredients and are a filling replacement for meat in recipes. To save even more on mushrooms, I buy whole mushrooms and slice them myself.

1 tbsp (15 ml) olive oil

¼ cup (40 g) diced onion

¼ cup (38 g) diced bell pepper

2 cups (140 g) diced white button mushrooms

2 tsp (6 g) Taco Seasoning Mix* (page 184)

1 cup (250 g) cooked black beans

2 cups (470 ml) Enchilada Sauce* (page 188)

12 to 14 corn tortillas*

1½ cups (180 g) shredded cheddar cheese

1½ cups (180 g) shredded Monterey Jack cheese

Use gluten-free corn tortillas, Taco Seasoning Mix and Enchilada Sauce to make these enchiladas gluten-free.

Preheat the oven to 350°F (180°C, or gas mark 4).

Heat the oil in a skillet. Add the onion, bell pepper and mushrooms. Sauté for 5 minutes, or until the onions are tender.

Stir the taco seasoning and black beans into the mushroom mixture. Cook over medium heat for 4 to 5 minutes, or until the beans are heated through.

Heat the enchilada sauce on the stove top in a small saucepan or in a bowl in the microwave for 1 to 2 minutes.

Heat the tortillas in the microwave for a minute to soften them up and make them more pliable.

Spread ½ cup (120 ml) of the enchilada sauce in the bottom of a 9 x 13-inch (23 x 33-cm) casserole dish.

Pour enough enchilada sauce onto a dinner plate to make a puddle. Place a tortilla on the plate and then flip it over, so that it is completely coated in enchilada sauce, then spoon the bean and mushroom mixture slightly to one side of the center. Sprinkle a tablespoon (8 g) of each cheese over the bean and mushroom mixture. Roll the tortilla to close and place seam side down in the casserole dish. Repeat with the rest of the tortillas.

Once you have finished filling the tortillas, pour the remaining enchilada sauce over the enchiladas. Sprinkle the remaining cheese over the enchiladas.

Place the casserole dish in the oven and bake for 15 minutes.

PREP-AHEAD TIP: The enchiladas can be assembled ahead of time and stored in the refrigerator for 1 or 2 days or in the freezer for up to 3 months.

TUSCAN WHITE BEAN AND ACORN SQUASH SOUP

BEST BATCH-COOKING METHOD: Any

Serves: 6

This hearty soup is brimming with flavor. To easily peel and chop an acorn squash, first cut it in half vertically, then scoop out the seeds. Then cut in the valleys to cut the two halves into wedges. Peel each wedge and then cut it into bite-size pieces. If you can't find acorn squash, feel free to substitute butternut squash or another mild winter squash.

The acorn squash seeds can be saved and roasted like pumpkin seeds. Roasted squash seeds make a tasty alternative to croutons on salads and in soups.

---

1 tbsp (15 ml) olive oil

1 cup (160 g) diced onion

4 cloves garlic, minced

4 cups (940 ml) Vegetable Broth* (page 193)

2 cups (400 g) peeled and diced acorn squash

1 tsp oregano

1 tsp basil

½ tsp thyme

¼ tsp rosemary

Pinch of salt

3½ cups (875 g) cooked cannellini beans

2 cups (140 g) torn fresh kale

* Use gluten-free Vegetable Broth to make this soup gluten-free.

Heat the olive oil in a large pot. Add the onion and garlic and sauté until the onion is tender, approximately 5 minutes.

Add the broth, acorn squash, oregano, basil, thyme, rosemary and salt to the pot. Cook over medium-high heat until it reaches a boil. Lower the heat and simmer for 10 minutes.

Add the beans and kale and simmer for 10 minutes longer.

PREP-AHEAD TIP: You can dice the onion and tear the kale 2 or 3 days ahead of time and store them in sealed containers in the refrigerator.

Serves:
6-8

MEDITERRANEAN BEANS AND RICE

BEST BATCH-COOKING METHOD: Any

The homemade Greek dressing infuses this easy dish with vibrant flavor. It can be served warm or chilled, though my family prefers it cold served over a bed of salad greens.

Beans and Rice

2 cups (500 g) cooked cannellini beans

2 cups (330 g) cooked rice

1 cup (100 g) thinly sliced black olives

½ cup (80 g) diced red onion

1 stalk celery, thinly sliced

Greek Dressing

¼ cup (60 ml) red wine vinegar

3 tbsp (45 ml) olive oil

1 tsp oregano

1 tsp basil

1 tsp garlic powder

½ tsp Dijon mustard*

½ tsp onion powder

¼ tsp Seasoned Salt* (page 183)

Pinch of coarsely ground pepper

Use gluten-free mustard and Seasoned Salt to make this recipe gluten-free.

To make the beans and rice, in a medium bowl or saucepan, combine the beans, rice, olive slices, onion and celery.

To make the dressing, in a cruet or lidded container, combine the vinegar, oil, oregano, basil, garlic powder, Dijon mustard, onion powder, salt and pepper. Shake well to mix.

Drizzle the dressing over the bean and rice mixture. Toss to coat.

If serving this dish warm, cook over low heat for 5 to 7 minutes, or until heated through. If you wish to serve it chilled, refrigerate for 1 to 2 hours before serving.

PREP-AHEAD TIP: You can assemble this beans and rice dish ahead of time and store it in a sealed container in the refrigerator for 2 or 3 days. The dressing can also be made ahead of time and stored in the refrigerator for 3 to 5 days. You can double or triple the dressing recipe to use on salads throughout the week.

SOUTHWEST THREE-BEAN SALAD

Serves: 8+

BEST BATCH-COOKING METHOD: Any

This is a flavorful twist on traditional three-bean salads and makes a great side dish for barbecues and picnics. The green beans and wax beans are replaced with cannellini and black beans. Then the bean salad is coated with a spicy honey-lime dressing.

1¾ cups (438 g) cooked black beans

1¾ cups (438 g) cooked kidney beans

1¾ cups (438 g) cooked cannellini beans

2 cups (300 g) grape or cherry tomatoes

½ cup (80 g) diced red onion

1 cup (150 g) diced bell pepper

3 tbsp (45 ml) olive oil

3 tbsp (45 ml) apple cider vinegar

3 tbsp (45 ml) lime juice

2 tbsp (30 ml) honey

1 tbsp (8 g) Taco Seasoning Mix* (page 184)

Use gluten-free Taco Seasoning Mix to make this salad gluten-free.

Add the beans, tomatoes, onion and bell pepper to a large bowl. Toss to combine.

In a small bowl, combine the olive oil, apple cider vinegar, lime juice, honey and taco seasoning mix. Stir well until mixed. If the honey is hard to stir, heat the mixture in the microwave for 20 seconds and then stir.

Drizzle the honey-lime dressing over the bean salad. Toss to coat.

Refrigerate the bean salad for at least 2 hours before serving.

NOTE: To save money, pick up extra limes when they are on sale. Squeeze the limes and measure the juice by the tablespoon (15 ml) into ice-cube trays. Once the lime juice cubes are frozen, store them in a sealable freezer bag and use them in recipes that call for fresh lime juice.

PREP-AHEAD TIP: This salad can be made ahead of time and stored in the refrigerator overnight.

PASTA E FAGIOLI WITH TORTELLINI AND KALE

Serves: 4–6

BEST BATCH-COOKING METHOD: Any

Pasta e fagioli is a meatless Italian dish made with pasta and beans. Instead of using a small pasta like ditalini, I like to use cheese tortellini to add another layer of flavor and make it even more filling. I add frozen tortellini in the last step and let it cook directly in the soup.

1 tbsp (15 ml) olive oil

1 cup (160 g) diced onion

3 cloves garlic, minced

2 stalks celery, thinly sliced

3 cups (705 ml) Vegetable Broth* (page 193)

1 tsp oregano

½ tsp rosemary

½ tsp thyme

1¾ cups (315 g) or 1 (14.5-oz [406-g]) can diced tomatoes

1¾ cups (438 g) cooked cannellini beans

2 cups (140 g) chopped fresh kale

16-oz (455-g) bag frozen tortellini*

* Use gluten-free Vegetable Broth and gluten-free tortellini to make this dish gluten-free.

Heat the olive oil in a large pot. Add the onion, garlic and celery. Sauté for 5 minutes, or until the onion is tender.

Add the broth, spices and tomatoes to the pot. Cook over high heat until it reaches a boil. Lower heat and add the beans and kale. Simmer for 10 minutes.

Add the frozen tortellini and cook for 6 to 8 minutes longer, or until the tortellini are heated through.

PREP-AHEAD TIP: You can make the pasta e fagioli in advance, but wait to add the tortellini until you are getting ready to reheat and serve it. Once the pasta is added it will continue to absorb liquid and expand, so the tortellini could begin to break apart if you add it too far in advance of serving this dish.

SOUTHWEST RICE SALAD WITH AVOCADO

BEST BATCH-COOKING METHOD: Any

This cold salad makes a delicious side dish, or you can serve it over a bed of greens and make a meal of it. Make sure the avocado pieces are coated with the dressing to help prevent them from browning while the salad is chilling.

Salad

2 cups (330 g) cooked rice

1 (15-oz [425-g]) can corn, drained

½ cup (80 g) diced red onion

½ cup (75 g) diced bell pepper

1 cup (150 g) cherry or grape tomatoes

1 or 2 avocados, peeled, pitted and diced

⅓ cup (40 g) shredded cheddar cheese

⅓ cup (40 g) shredded Monterey Jack cheese

Dressing

¼ cup (60 ml) Ranch Salad Dressing* (page 187)

2 tbsp (30 ml) lime juice

2 tbsp (30 ml) olive oil

2 tbsp (30 ml) honey

2 tsp (6 g) Taco Seasoning Mix* (page 184)

Use gluten-free Ranch Salad Dressing and Taco Seasoning Mix to make this salad gluten-free.

To make the salad, in a medium bowl, combine the rice, corn, onion, bell pepper, tomatoes, avocado and cheese.

To make the dressing, in a small bowl, combine the ranch dressing, lime juice, oil, honey and taco seasoning mix. Stir well to combine.

Pour the dressing over the salad. Toss to thoroughly coat. Refrigerate for 1 to 2 hours before serving.

PREP-AHEAD TIP: If you want to make the salad a day or two in advance, wait to add the avocado right before serving.

BLACK BEAN AND SWEET POTATO BURRITOS

Serves: 8

BEST BATCH-COOKING METHOD: Any

I know it sounds like a crazy combination, but stick with me. The blend of spicy black beans and sweet potatoes really does work. My friend Laura H. of The View from the Treehouse introduced me to the idea of combining beans and sweet potatoes. I was skeptical at first, but found the pairing delicious. I now look for new and unusual ways to combine sweet potatoes with beans.

1 cup (225 g) mashed cooked sweet potatoes or 1 large uncooked sweet potato

1 tbsp (15 ml) olive oil

½ cup (80 g) diced onion

2 cloves garlic, minced

2 cups (500 g) cooked black beans

4 tsp (10 g) Taco Seasoning Mix* (page 184)

1 cup (120 g) shredded cheddar cheese

8 soft tortillas*

* Use gluten-free Taco Seasoning Mix and gluten-free tortillas to make these burritos gluten-free.

If you don't have a baked sweet potato on hand, you can steam a large sweet potato. Put 2 inches (5 cm) of water in a pot and bring it to a boil. Peel a sweet potato and cut it into bite-size pieces. Place it in a steamer basket and steam for 15 to 20 minutes, or until it is tender enough to mash. You can mash the sweet potato pieces with a potato masher or use an immersion blender. If it seems too dry, add a little water from the pot you used to steam the sweet potatoes.

Preheat the oven to 350°F (180°C, or gas mark 4).

Heat the oil in a skillet. Add the onion and sauté for 4 minutes. Add the garlic and sauté for 1 minute.

Add the beans and taco seasoning to the onions and mix well. Cook over medium heat for 3 to 4 minutes, or until the beans are heated through.

Spread 2 tablespoons (28 g) of sweet potato on each tortilla. Top with ¼ cup (62 g) of the bean mixture. Sprinkle 2 tablespoons (16 g) of cheddar cheese over the beans. Then fold the top and bottom of the tortilla toward the center, fold one side toward the middle, and roll to close.

Place the burritos in a baking dish and bake for 15 minutes.

PREP-AHEAD TIP: You can bake or steam the sweet potatoes in advance. You can also make the bean mixture a day or two ahead of time. Then you can quickly assemble the burritos and bake them on busy weeknights.

Serves: 4

LENTIL AND RICE TACOS

BEST BATCH-COOKING METHOD: Any

Lentils make a great substitute for ground beef in recipes. They are high in protein and their small size works well in place of the small crumbles of cooked ground beef. Even better, you can buy a pound (455 g) of dried lentils for about a fourth of the price of a pound (455 g) of ground beef.

1 tbsp (15 ml) olive oil

½ cup (80 g) diced onion

¼ cup (38 g) diced bell pepper

2 cloves garlic, minced

1 cup (250 g) cooked lentils

1 cup (165 g) cooked brown rice

1¾ cups (315 g) or 14.5-oz (406-g) can diced tomatoes

2 tsp (6 g) Taco Seasoning Mix* (page 184)

8 tortillas*

2 cups (140 g) shredded lettuce

1 cup (120 g) shredded cheese

1 avocado, peeled, pitted, and sliced (optional)

Salsa (optional)

* Use gluten-free tortillas and Taco Seasoning Mix to make this dish gluten-free.

Heat the olive oil in a skillet or frying pan. Add the onion and bell pepper and sauté for 4 minutes. Add the garlic and sauté for 1 more minute.

Add the lentils, rice, tomatoes and taco seasoning. Mix well. Cook over medium heat for 4 to 5 minutes, or until the lentils are heated through. The vegetables should release some liquid as they cook, but if you don't feel there is enough liquid, add 1 to 2 tablespoons (15 to 30 ml) of water.

Heat the tortillas in the microwave for 1 minute to make them more pliable. Add 1 minute more if necessary.

Spoon the lentils and rice mixture into the tortillas and top with the lettuce, cheese, avocado and salsa. Repeat until you have made all the tacos you need.

PREP-AHEAD TIP: You can make the lentil and rice taco filling in advance and store it in the refrigerator for 2 or 3 days.

15-MINUTE REFRIED BLACK BEANS

BEST BATCH-COOKING METHOD: Any

Serves: 4–6

I grew up on traditional refried beans cooked in lard, but I also grew up with a wood-burning stove that we could cook the beans on for hours while heating our home. Now it seems indulgent to cook beans on the stove top for hours just to make refried beans. This quick and easy bean recipe saves not only time but also energy. You can use these refried black beans as a side dish or in recipes such as burritos and tostadas.

1 tbsp (15 ml) olive oil

½ cup (80 g) diced onion

2 cloves garlic, minced

3 to 3½ cups (750 to 875 g) cooked black beans

1 tsp Taco Seasoning Mix* (page 184), optional

⅛ tsp Seasoned Salt* (page 183)

Pinch of pepper

¼ cup (60 ml) Vegetable Broth* (page 193), as needed

* Use gluten-free Taco Seasoning Mix, Seasoned Salt and Vegetable Broth to make these beans gluten-free.

Heat the olive oil in a skillet over medium heat.

Add the onion and sauté for 4 minutes. Add the garlic and cook for 1 more minute.

Stir the black beans, taco seasoning, salt and pepper into the onion mixture. Cook over low heat until the beans are thoroughly heated, about 5 minutes. Stir occasionally.

Use a potato masher or the back of a spatula to smash the black beans to the desired texture while cooking over low heat. Add the broth as needed to achieve the desired consistency.

PREP-AHEAD TIP: This recipe can be made ahead of time and stored in the refrigerator for 3 or 4 days.

15-MINUTE "BAKED" BEANS

BEST BATCH-COOKING METHOD: Any

Serves: 6–8

I love baked beans, but I do not like the idea of heating up the house while baking them for 4 to 8 hours. So I came up with this cheater recipe that allows me to make them in a fraction of the time.

Confession: I never liked the floating blob of bacon fat on top of traditional baked beans, so I crumble cooked bacon into my beans to add flavor. You can leave the bacon out to make vegetarian baked beans.

---

1 tbsp (15 ml) olive oil

¼ cup (40 g) diced red onion

½ cup (120 g) tomato sauce

¼ cup (60 ml) maple syrup

3 tbsp (45 g) brown sugar

3 tbsp (45 ml) molasses

2 tbsp (30 ml) apple cider vinegar

1 tsp dried mustard

1 tsp smoked paprika

⅛ tsp Seasoned Salt* (page 183)

Pinch of pepper

3 cups (750 g) cooked white beans or navy beans

1 slice cooked bacon (page 47), crumbled

* Use gluten-free Seasoned Salt the make these beans gluten-free.

Heat the oil in a large saucepan. Add the onion and sauté until tender, approximately 5 minutes.

Add the tomato sauce, maple syrup, brown sugar, molasses, vinegar, dried mustard, paprika, salt and pepper. Stir to mix well.

Add the beans and bacon. Bring to a boil, then lower the heat and simmer for 10 minutes.

PREP-AHEAD TIP: You can make the beans in advance and store them in the refrigerator for 2 or 3 days. Reheat over medium-low heat.

MEXICAN RICE

BEST BATCH-COOKING METHOD: Any

This zesty Mexican rice recipe has a lot of flavor with a bit of a bite to it. You can reduce the amount of jalapeño peppers if you prefer a milder Mexican rice.

Although I usually serve this as a side dish, occasionally we just make a meal of the rice and 15-Minute Refried Black Beans (page 135).

1 tbsp (15 ml) olive oil

½ cup (80 g) diced onion

¼ cup (38 g) diced bell pepper

1 jalapeño pepper, seeded and diced

2 cloves garlic, minced

1¾ cups (315 g) or 14.5-oz (406-g) can diced tomatoes

3 cups (495 g) cooked rice

1½ tsp (3 g) ground cumin

1 tsp oregano

½ tsp ground coriander (optional)

⅛ tsp Seasoned Salt* (page 183)

2 tbsp (30 ml) Vegetable Broth* (page 193), if needed

Use gluten-free Seasoned Salt and broth to make this rice gluten-free.

Heat the olive oil in large saucepan or skillet. Add the onion, peppers and garlic. Sauté for 5 minutes, or until the onion is tender.

Add the tomatoes, rice and spices. Stir well.

Cook over medium-low heat, stirring occasionally, for 5 minutes, or until the rice is heated through. The tomatoes should release liquid as they cook, but if the rice seems too dry add a little vegetable broth.

PREP-AHEAD TIP: You can make this rice in advance and store it in the refrigerator in a sealed container for 1 or 2 days.

VEGETABLE FRIED RICE LETTUCE WRAPS

BEST BATCH-COOKING METHOD: Any

Fried rice is usually relegated to being the base for a fancy Asian dish. My family enjoys fried rice so much that they can and will make a meal of it alone. After the rice is finished cooking, you can divide it among large romaine lettuce leaves for a quick and easy meal.

1 tbsp (15 ml) mild-flavored oil

4 green onions, thinly sliced

1 cup (130 g) matchstick-cut carrot

1 cup (130 g) frozen peas

3 cups (495 g) cooked rice

1 cup (50 g) bean sprouts

¼ cup (60 ml) soy sauce*

3 tbsp (45 ml) orange juice

1 tsp honey

4 large romaine lettuce leaves

* Use gluten-free soy sauce or coconut aminos to make this dish gluten-free.

Heat the oil in a large skillet. Add the green onions, carrots and peas. Cook over medium-high heat for 4 to 5 minutes, or until the onion is tender.

Add the rice, bean sprouts, soy sauce, orange juice and honey to the pan. Cook, stirring, for 3 to 4 minutes, or until the liquid has been absorbed and the sprouts are tender.

Remove from the heat and let sit for a minute.

Divide the fried rice among the lettuce leaves. You can wrap them and eat them like a burrito or fold them over and eat them like a taco.

PREP-AHEAD TIP: You can slice the green onions and carrots in advance. The green onions can be stored in a sealed container or resealable bag in the refrigerator for 1 or 2 days. The carrot slices can be stored for 2 or 3 days in a sealed container with a moist paper towel.

ITALIAN RICE SALAD
WITH ARTICHOKE HEARTS

BEST BATCH-COOKING METHOD: Any

This is a hearty alternative to a garden salad. I like to serve it on a bed of greens: the dressing from the rice salad trickles down and coats the lettuce.

1 (12-oz [340-g]) bag frozen artichoke hearts, thawed

2 cups (300 g) cherry or grape tomatoes

½ cup (75 g) diced bell pepper

½ cup (80 g) diced onion

½ cup (120 ml) Italian Salad Dressing* (page 186)

4 cups (660 g) cooked rice

Use gluten-free Italian Salad Dressing to make this salad gluten-free.

Place the thawed artichoke hearts, tomatoes, bell pepper and onion in a large bowl.

Drizzle the salad dressing over the vegetables. Toss to coat.

Stir in the rice until it is fully incorporated.

Refrigerate for 2 hours before serving.

PREP-AHEAD TIP: You can dice the bell pepper and onion in advance and store them in the refrigerator for 2 or 3 days. You can also make the Italian Salad Dressing 4 or 5 days ahead of time.

Serves: 4

RATATOUILLE RICE SKILLET

BEST BATCH-COOKING METHOD: Any

My kids used to pile their ratatouille onto a bed of rice and then pour Italian dressing over the top. I decided that since they liked it that way so much, I might as well save time and dishes by combining the rice, vegetables and dressing into an easy one-dish dinner.

2 cups (160 g) cubed eggplant

Salt

½ cup (120 ml) Italian Salad Dressing (page 186), divided

½ cup (80 g) coarsely chopped onion

¼ cup (38 g) coarsely chopped green bell pepper

2 cloves garlic, minced

1 medium zucchini, sliced ¼-inch (6-mm) thick

2 small yellow squash, sliced ¼-inch (6-mm) thick

2 Roma tomatoes, seeded and cut into bite-size pieces

1 cup (70 g) chopped mushrooms

4 cups (660 g) cooked rice

Use gluten-free Italian Salad Dressing to make this dish gluten-free.

After cutting the eggplant into bite-size pieces, place it in a colander, sprinkle it with salt and let it sit while you prep the other ingredients. Before you cook the eggplant, rinse it and pat it dry.

Add 2 tablespoons (30 ml) of the Italian dressing to a large skillet. Add the chopped onion, pepper and garlic. Sauté for 5 minutes, or until the onion is tender.

Add the eggplant and 1 tablespoon (15 ml) of the salad dressing. Cook for 5 minutes over medium heat, stirring occasionally.

Add the zucchini, yellow squash and 1 tablespoon (15 ml) salad dressing. Cook for another 5 minutes, stirring occasionally.

Add the chopped tomato, sliced mushrooms, rice and remaining ¼ cup (60 ml) salad dressing. Cook for an additional 5 minutes, or until the mushrooms are tender and the rice is heated through.

PREP-AHEAD TIP: You can make the dressing ahead of time and store it in the refrigerator for 4 or 5 days. The onion and bell pepper can be chopped 2 or 3 days in advance. The tomato and mushrooms can be chopped 1 or 2 days in advance. The zucchini and squash can be chopped in 1 or 2 days in advance, but toss it with a little dressing before you store it to keep it from discoloring.

VEGETARIAN SLOPPY JOE STUFFED EGGPLANT

BEST BATCH-COOKING METHOD: Any

Japanese and Chinese eggplants are long and thin, about the size of a medium zucchini. This makes them the perfect size for creating stuffed eggplant "boats." They are also milder in flavor and less bitter than other eggplants, so you don't have to salt the eggplant before cooking it.

4 Japanese or Chinese eggplants

1 tbsp (15 ml) olive oil

½ cup (80 g) diced onion

2 tbsp (18 g) diced red bell pepper

1 stalk celery, diced

1 cup (120 g) diced zucchini

3 cloves garlic, minced

1 cup (70 g) diced mushrooms

2 cups (500 g) cooked lentils

1 cup (245 g) tomato sauce

1 tbsp (15 ml) apple cider vinegar

1 tbsp (15 ml) Worcestershire sauce*

3 tbsp (45 g) brown sugar

2 tsp (6 g) ground mustard

1 tsp smoked paprika

1 cup (120 g) shredded mozzarella cheese

* Use gluten-free Worcestershire sauce to make this dish gluten-free.

Cut the eggplants in half lengthwise and scoop out the seeds.

Preheat the oven to 350°F (180°C, or gas mark 4) and grease a baking dish.

Add the oil, onion, red pepper, celery and zucchini to a large skillet. Sauté for 4 minutes. Add the garlic and mushrooms and sauté for 2 more minutes.

Add the lentils, tomato sauce, vinegar, Worcestershire sauce, sugar, mustard and paprika to the skillet. Stir well to combine the ingredients. Bring to a boil. Lower the heat and simmer for 5 minutes.

Spoon the Sloppy Joe mixture into the eggplants. Sprinkle the mozzarella cheese over the top of the eggplant and place the eggplants in the greased baking dish.

Bake for 25 minutes, or until the eggplants are tender when pierced with a fork.

PREP-AHEAD TIP: You can make the Sloppy Joe mixture in advance and store it in the refrigerator for 2 or 3 days.

CAJUN RED BEANS AND RICE WRAPS

Serves: 8

BEST BATCH-COOKING METHOD: Any

One of the great things about cooking dried beans is there are so many more varieties available to you. Although red beans are common in the South, in most of the United States the only place you can find them is in the dried beans section. If you can't find red beans, you can substitute kidney beans in this recipe.

1 tbsp (15 ml) olive oil

½ cup (80 g) diced onion

½ cup (75 g) diced bell pepper

1 stalk celery, thinly sliced

2 cloves garlic, minced

2 cups (500 g) cooked red beans

2 cups (330 g) cooked brown rice

1 tbsp (8 g) Cajun Seasoning Mix*
(page 183)

¼ cup (60 ml) Vegetable Broth*
(page 193) or water

8 soft tortillas*

2 cups (140 g) spinach leaves

2 Roma tomatoes, sliced

* Use gluten-free tortillas, Cajun Seasoning Mix and Vegetable Broth to make this recipe gluten-free.

Heat the oil in a large skillet. Add the onion, bell pepper, celery and garlic. Sauté for 5 minutes, or until the onion is tender.

Add the beans, rice, Cajun seasoning mix and broth. Stir to combine. Cook over medium heat for 5 minutes, or until the beans are heated through.

Heat the tortillas in the microwave if necessary to make them more pliable.

Place ¼ cup (17 g) of spinach leaves on each tortilla slightly to one side of the center. Top with ½ cup (125 g) of Cajun beans and rice. Top with the tomato slices.

Fold the top and bottom of the tortilla toward the center. Fold the short side toward the center and keep rolling to close.

PREP-AHEAD TIP: You can dice the onion and bell pepper ahead of time and store them in the refrigerator for 2 or 3 days. You can also slice the celery in advance and store it in the refrigerator for 2 or 3 days or in the freezer for up to 3 months.

INDIAN CHICKPEAS AND RICE

BEST BATCH-COOKING METHOD: Any

Serves: 4

One day my daughter jokingly challenged me to create a recipe that used as many spices that began with the letter C as possible. At the time I laughed off the challenge. Later that day I was getting ready to make an Indian dish and discovered I was out of garam masala. I realized it was the perfect time to see how many spices I could use that began with the letter C instead of sending my long-suffering husband to the store to buy the missing ingredient.

Whenever I am missing an ingredient for a recipe, I always look through my pantry and try to find a substitution instead of making a store run for one ingredient. All of the recipes in this cookbook are quite flexible and can be easily adapted in a pinch.

I keep cardamom on hand to use in homemade chai. If you don't have it, leave it out or replace it with extra cinnamon.

1 tbsp (15 ml) olive oil

½ cup (80 g) diced onion

2 cloves garlic, minced

1¾ cups (438 g) cooked chickpeas

1¾ cups (315 g) or 1 (14.5-oz [406-g]) can diced tomatoes

2 tsp (6 g) curry powder

1 bay leaf

1 tsp grated ginger

½ tsp ground cinnamon

½ tsp ground cardamom

½ tsp ground coriander

¼ tsp nutmeg

⅛ tsp ground cloves

Pinch of cayenne pepper

2 cups (330 g) cooked rice

Heat the olive oil in a skillet. Add the onion and sauté for 4 minutes. Add the garlic and cook for 1 minute.

Add the chickpeas, tomatoes and spices. Bring to a boil, then lower the heat and simmer for 5 minutes.

Serve over rice.

PREP-AHEAD TIP: You can dice the onions 2 or 3 days in advance and dice the tomatoes 1 or 2 days ahead of time and store them in sealed containers in the refrigerator.

VEGETARIAN STUFFED PEPPER SOUP

BEST BATCH-COOKING METHOD: Any

Stuffed peppers are delicious, but bell peppers are very expensive when they are not in season. This stuffed pepper soup allows us to enjoy the flavors of stuffed peppers for a fraction of the cost any time of year.

1 tbsp (15 ml) olive oil

1 cup (160 g) diced onion

1 cup (150 g) diced bell pepper

4 cloves garlic, minced

1¾ cups (315 g) or 1 (14.5-oz [406-g]) can diced tomatoes

1¾ cups (430 ml) tomato sauce or 1 (15 oz [425 ml]) can tomato sauce

1 cup (235 ml) Vegetable Broth* (page 193)

4 tsp (15 g) sugar

2 tsp (3 g) oregano

2 tsp (3 g) basil

1 tsp cumin

1 tsp thyme

Pinch of salt

1¾ cups (438 g) white beans

2 cups (330 g) cooked rice

Use gluten-free Vegetable Broth to make this recipe gluten-free.

Add the oil to a large skillet. Add the onion and bell pepper and sauté for 4 minutes. Add the garlic and sauté for 1 minute.

Add the diced tomatoes, tomato sauce, broth, sugar and spices. Stir well to combine. Bring to a boil. Lower the heat and simmer for 10 minutes.

Add the beans and rice and simmer for 5 minutes longer.

PREP-AHEAD TIP: You can make this soup in advance as long as you leave the rice out. The rice will absorb extra liquid, so wait until you are reheating the soup to add the cooked rice.

Flavorful Vegetables in Minutes

Fresh vegetables are sometimes erroneously described as expensive. In my experience, they are only expensive if you are buying them when they are not locally in season. Eating in-season produce will not only save you money, but it will also ensure you are consuming higher quality, more nutrient-dense produce.

You can find great deals on fresh produce at your local farmers' market, warehouse stores and local food co-ops. You can also save money on produce by watching for sales at your local store.

If a fruit or vegetable is usually featured in a particular cuisine, look for it at an appropriate ethnic food market. My local grocery store usually has eight hard mangoes in stock and sells them for $1.50 each, but if I go to the Asian market, they have a large bin of ripe mangoes often priced as low as three for $1.00.

If you absolutely must have a certain out-of-season vegetable for a dish or to fill a craving, consider buying it from the freezer section. Frozen vegetables are flash-frozen at the peak of freshness. Not only are frozen vegetables more frugal, but also blanching and then rapidly freezing vegetables helps produce retain its fresh taste, texture, appearance and many of its nutrients. Most frozen vegetables can be stored for 9 to 12 months.

If you find a great deal on produce, you can stock up on it and freeze it yourself, but you should compare how much frozen vegetables sell for in your area and analyze whether it makes sense to buy vegetables and flash-freeze them yourself. If you have a garden, it definitely pays to freeze your excess produce.

To blanch vegetables, submerge them in boiling water for 1 to 5 minutes depending on the vegetable, then quickly remove them from the boiling water and place in a bowl of ice water to quickly cool. Once they have cooled, pat them dry before freezing them in freezer bags. Be sure to remove as much air as possible from the containers. Check the recommended blanching guidelines for any vegetables you wish to freeze (see page 150).

Most of the vegetable recipes in this chapter can be made in 15 to 20 minutes, so you can quickly cook a side dish while you are preparing your main entrée. You can speed the prep time on many of the vegetable dishes by washing and cutting the vegetables a day or two in advance. Vegetables such as potatoes that will discolor after being peeled or cut can be stored in a bowl of water in the refrigerator. Vegetables that easily dry out after being cut can be stored in a container with a moistened paper towel.

On really busy weeks, you can save time by batch cooking vegetables in advance. Choose heartier vegetables that can stand being reheated, such as cauliflower, root vegetables, green beans, Brussels sprouts and snap peas. When you cook them ahead of time, instead of cooking them until they are fork-tender, stop a little bit earlier than that. On the night you wish to serve them, finish cooking them in the skillet or in the oven. Vegetables cooked on the stove top should be ready in about 5 minutes and vegetables cooked in the oven will be done in about 10 minutes.

MAKE A LARGE SALAD AHEAD OF TIME

Combine shredded lettuce, shredded carrots and cherry tomatoes. You can also add radish and green onion slices if you wish. Place a paper towel on top of the bowl before closing it to absorb the excess moisture. The salad can be used as a base for a fast and easy dinner on a busy night or as an easy side dish. Plate the salad and then add dressing instead of adding dressing to the bowl. Dressing will wilt the uneaten greens, rendering any leftover salad inedible.

RECOMMENDED BLANCHING TIMES FOR VEGETABLES

Although this list of blanching times is not comprehensive, it does cover many of the vegetables commonly used in this cookbook. There are some vegetables that I do not blanch before freezing. I dice tomatoes and freeze them in 1¾-cup (315-g) quantities without blanching or removing the skins. I also dice and freeze onions and celery without blanching. If I can't use mushrooms before they will turn, I sauté them in oil or butter and then freeze the cooked mushrooms in usable quantities.[1]

VEGETABLE	TIME
Asparagus (thin stalks)	2 minutes
Asparagus (medium stalks)	3 minutes
Asparagus (thick stalks)	4 minutes
Broccoli florets	3 minutes
Carrots (sliced or diced)	2 minutes
Cauliflower florets	3 minutes
Green beans	3 minutes
Green peas	1½ minutes
Peppers (strips)	2 minutes
Potatoes (diced)	3 minutes
Snap peas	3 minutes

1 For the recommended blanching times, I consulted: *So Easy to Preserve*, 5th ed. 2006. Bulletin 989, Cooperative Extension Service, The University of Georgia, Athens. Revised by Elizabeth L. Andress, PhD, and Judy A. Harrison, PhD, Extension Foods Specialists.

SAVORY MASHED SWEET POTATOES

Although you can make mashed sweet potatoes with boiled diced sweet potatoes, I prefer to make them with baked sweet potatoes, as I find it makes a smoother final product.

3 medium sweet potatoes

4 tbsp (56 g) butter or (60 ml) olive oil

2 tsp (3 g) thyme

1 tsp garlic powder

1 tsp rosemary

Preheat the oven to 400°F (200°C, or gas mark 6).

Pierce the sweet potatoes and place them on a baking sheet. Bake for 45 minutes, or until fork-tender.

Remove the skin from the sweet potatoes and place the sweet potatoes in a large mixing bowl. If you are going to stuff the potato skin, cut an oval in the top of the sweet potato and scoop out the flesh.

Mash the sweet potatoes with a fork or potato masher.

Add the butter and spices and mix with a hand mixer until smooth and creamy.

PREP-AHEAD TIP: You can bake the sweet potatoes the night before to cut down on prep time during the dinnertime rush. After you have scooped out the sweet potato flesh, you can stuff the sweet potato skins with chili (page 89) or pulled pork (page 46).

CINNAMON-GLAZED CARROTS

The natural sweetness of carrots pairs well with traditional baking spices. You can easily vary this recipe by replacing the cinnamon with Pumpkin Pie Spice Mix (page 185) or apple pie spice mix.

1 tbsp (14 g) butter

1 tbsp (12 g) sugar

½ tsp cinnamon

½ cup (120 ml) water, plus more as needed

1 lb (455 g) carrots, sliced ½-inch (1.3-cm) thick

Melt the butter in a large skillet.

Add the sugar, cinnamon and water to the butter. Stir until the sugar is dissolved.

Add the carrot slices and stir to coat. Cook over medium heat, stirring occasionally, until the carrots are fork-tender, approximately 10 minutes.

If all of the liquid is cooked off before the carrots are done cooking, add 1 to 2 tablespoons (15 to 30 ml) more water.

PREP-AHEAD TIP: You can cut the carrots 1 or 2 days in advance. Store the cut carrots in a plastic bag with a moist paper towel to keep them from drying out.

Serves: 4

CAJUN-SPICED CAULIFLOWER

Since cauliflower is so mild, it creates a perfect base for whatever seasonings you want to coat it with. The Cajun Seasoning Mix (page 183) lends a flavorful kick to the cauliflower without adding too much heat. This dish makes an excellent substitute for fries.

1 head cauliflower

2 tbsp (30 ml) olive oil

1 tbsp (8 g) Cajun Seasoning Mix* (page 183)

* Use gluten-free Cajun Seasoning Mix to make this gluten-free.

Preheat the oven to 450°F (230°C, or gas mark 8).

Cut the cauliflower into bite-size pieces and place them in a large baking dish or on a cookie sheet with raised sides.

Drizzle the olive oil over the cauliflower. Toss to thoroughly coat the cauliflower florets. Sprinkle the spices over the cauliflower and toss until the pieces are well covered with the spices.

Bake for 20 minutes, or until the cauliflower is fork-tender.

PREP-AHEAD TIP: You can cut the cauliflower into florets a day in advance and store them in a large resealable bag in the refrigerator.

ASPARAGUS WITH BALSAMIC GLAZE AND CHIVES

The tangy balsamic glaze enhances the flavor of the asparagus without overpowering it. When asparagus is in season and affordable, we enjoy it frequently. Once asparagus season is over and the price goes back up, I either use frozen asparagus or substitute whole green beans for the asparagus in this recipe.

1 tbsp (15 ml) olive oil

¼ cup (12 g) thinly sliced chives

2 cloves garlic, minced

1 tbsp (15 ml) balsamic vinegar

1½ tsp (6 g) sugar

1 lb (455 g) asparagus, cut into 1-inch (2.5-cm) pieces

Heat the olive oil in a skillet. Add the chives and garlic and sauté for 1 minute.

Stir the balsamic vinegar and sugar into the oil until the sugar is mostly dissolved.

Add the asparagus to the skillet and stir to coat.

Place a lid on the pan and reduce the heat to low. Simmer for 15 minutes, or until the asparagus is fork-tender.

PREP-AHEAD TIP: You can cut the asparagus 1 or 2 days ahead of time and store in a sealed container in the refrigerator until you are ready to cook.

ITALIAN ARTICHOKE HEARTS

This is so easy I almost feel bad sharing it, but it is too good to keep a secret. To make a quick and easy side dish, just cook artichoke hearts in Italian Salad Dressing.

1 (12-oz [340-g]) bag frozen artichokes, thawed

¼ cup (60 ml) Italian Salad Dressing* (page 186)

Use gluten-free Italian Salad Dressing to make this dish gluten-free.

Place the artichokes hearts in a skillet. Drizzle the dressing over the artichoke hearts. Toss to coat.

Cook over medium heat for 5 to 7 minutes, or until the artichoke hearts are heated through.

PREP-AHEAD TIP: Although I usually serve this as a side dish, you can add these Italian artichoke hearts to salads in place of traditional marinated artichokes if you wish. If using in a salad, you can cook the artichokes in advance and store in the refrigerator for 2 or 3 days. Add the chilled artichoke hearts directly to the salad.

GARLIC-GINGER GREEN BEANS

Serves: 4

When green beans are in season, I steam fresh ones to make this flavorful dish, but during the winter, I use whole frozen green beans. You can quickly thaw frozen green beans by running them under warm water. Whether you steam or thaw your green beans, make sure you pat them dry before using them in this recipe. You don't want to dilute the flavor of the spices with excess water.

1 lb (455 g) frozen or fresh whole green beans

2 tsp (10 ml) sesame oil or olive oil

1 tsp grated ginger

2 cloves garlic, minced

¼ cup (60 ml) soy sauce*

2 tsp (6 g) cornstarch

2 tsp (10 ml) mirin

1 tbsp (15 ml) honey

* Substitute gluten-free soy sauce to make this recipe gluten-free.

If using frozen green beans, thaw them by running them under hot water, then pat dry. If using fresh green beans, snap the stems off and steam them for 5 minutes.

Add the oil to a frying pan. Add the ginger and garlic and sauté for 1 to 2 minutes, or until the garlic just starts to brown.

Add the soy sauce and cornstarch to a small bowl and whisk to combine. Add the soy mixture to the ginger and garlic.

Add the mirin and honey to the soy mixture. Stir to combine. Cook over medium heat until the sauce thickens.

Add the green beans to the skillet and toss to coat with the sauce. Continue cooking over medium heat for 5 minutes, or until the green beans are heated through and fork-tender.

PREP-AHEAD TIP: If you are cooking with fresh green beans, you can steam them 1 or 2 days in advance. Pat them dry after steaming and store them in a lidded container until you are ready to cook with them.

BROILED HONEY MUSTARD BROCCOFLOWER

Broccoflower is a cross between broccoli and cauliflower. It has the texture of cauliflower and color of broccoli. It is more flavorful than cauliflower, but milder than broccoli. Some stores sell it as green cauliflower; by any name it is delicious and easy to work with. It pairs well with any number of savory spices, but for a special treat coat it in honey mustard sauce before broiling it.

1 head broccoflower, cut into bite-size pieces

1 tbsp (15 ml) olive oil

3 tbsp (33 g) mustard*

3 tbsp (45 ml) honey

* Use gluten-free mustard to make this dish gluten-free.

Preheat the oven to broil and cover the broiling pan with foil.

Spread the broccoflower pieces over the broiling pan.

In a small bowl, combine the oil, mustard and honey.

Drizzle the honey mustard sauce over the broccoflower pieces. Toss to coat the broccoflower florets thoroughly with the honey mustard sauce.

Place the pan with the broccoflower 6 inches (15 cm) below the heat source. Broil for 7 minutes, then toss to coat. Continue broiling for 8 more minutes, or until the broccoflower is browned and fork-tender.

PREP-AHEAD TIP: You can cut the broccoflower into florets a day in advance and store them in a large resealable bag in the refrigerator.

PUMPKIN PIE–SPICED PARSNIP FRIES

Parsnips are an often overlooked vegetable. They are less sweet and have a bit more spiciness to them than carrots. They are similar in texture, though, so you can cook them in many of the same recipes that you use carrots in, but you should tailor the spices to enhance their different flavor.

6 parsnips

2 tbsp (28 g) butter

2 tbsp (30 ml) honey

1 tbsp (8 g) Pumpkin Pie Spice Mix (page 185)

Preheat the oven to 450°F (230°C, or gas mark 8).

Peel the parsnips and cut into 2-inch (5-cm) wedges.

Place the parsnips on a baking tray.

Place the butter and honey in a small, microwave-safe bowl. Place in the microwave for 1 minute, or until the butter is melted.

Drizzle the butter mixture over the parsnips, then toss until the parsnip wedges are thoroughly coated. Sprinkle the pumpkin pie spice over the parsnips. Toss until the spices evenly coat the parsnips.

Bake for 10 minutes, then flip the fries over and bake for 10 to 15 minutes longer.

PREP-AHEAD Tip: The parsnips can be cut 1 or 2 days in advance and stored in a plastic bag with a moistened paper towel to keep them from drying out.

Serves: 6

ROASTED LEMON DIJON BROCCOLI

The pairing of lemon and Dijon mustard makes this broccoli side dish a stand-out. This dish is easy to prepare on busy nights.

8 cups (560 g) broccoli florets

¼ cup (60 ml) olive oil

1 tbsp (15 ml) lemon juice

1 tbsp (11 g) Dijon mustard*

1 tbsp (12 g) sugar

Use gluten-free mustard to make this dish gluten-free.

Preheat the oven to 400°F (200°C, or gas mark 6).

Place the broccoli florets on a baking sheet.

In a small bowl, combine the oil, lemon juice, Dijon mustard and sugar.

Drizzle the lemon Dijon mixture over the broccoli. Toss to thoroughly coat.

Roast the broccoli florets for 15 to 20 minutes, or until fork-tender.

PREP-AHEAD TIP: You can cut the broccoli into florets 1 or 2 days in advance and store them in a large resealable bag in the refrigerator.

Serves:
4-6

BUTTER TOSSED
BRUSSELS SPROUTS

You can cook just about any vegetable in butter and garlic and create a delicious side dish, and this includes Brussels sprouts. If you think you don't like Brussels sprouts, you were probably served boiled sprouts as a child. Cooking the Brussels sprouts in a skillet will sear the cut side, mellow the flavor and maybe just make you fall in love with these awesome veggies.

2 tbsp (28 g) butter

2 tbsp (30 ml) olive oil

4 cloves garlic, minced

20 Brussels sprouts, outer leaves removed and cut in half

Seasoned Salt* (page 183) and pepper to taste

Use gluten-free Seasoned Salt to make this dish gluten-free.

Melt the butter in a large skillet or frying pan with a lid. Add the oil and garlic and cook for 1 minute, or until the garlic is browned.

Add the Brussels sprouts to the skillet and toss to coat. Then place the Brussels sprouts cut side down in the pan. Sprinkle a little seasoned salt and coarsely ground pepper over the Brussels sprouts.

Place a lid on the pan and cook over medium heat for 12 to 15 minutes, or until the Brussels sprouts are fork-tender.

PREP-AHEAD Tip: You can remove the Brussels sprouts from the stock 2 or 3 days ahead of time and store the sprouts in a bowl in the refrigerator.

Serves: 6

PEAS AND CORN WITH BASIL

My daughter came up with this recipe by altering my mother-in-law's peas with basil recipe. This recipe is the reason my youngest son ended his boycott of peas, so it is now a regular on our dinner menu.

3 tbsp (42 g) butter

½ cup (80 g) diced onion

2 cups (260 g) fresh or frozen peas

2 cups (260 g) fresh or frozen corn kernels

1 tsp dried basil

Melt the butter in a large skillet. Add the onion and sauté until they are translucent, approximately 5 minutes.

Add the peas, corn and basil. Sauté over medium-low heat until the peas and corn are tender, approximately 5 minutes for frozen vegetables and 8 to 10 minutes for fresh vegetables.

PREP-AHEAD TIP: If you are using fresh corn and peas, you can cut the corn from the cob and shell the peas a day ahead of time and store them in a lidded container in the refrigerator.

Serves: 8

FRENCH ONION GREEN BEAN CASSEROLE

This is a delicious twist on the traditional green bean casserole. It combines the flavors of French onion soup with green bean casserole. This casserole takes a little longer to prepare, so I make it when cooking roast chicken for a special Sunday dinner. It is a forgiving dish; you can adjust the temperature and cooking time if you are cooking it along with something else in the oven.

¼ cup (56 g) butter

2 yellow onions, thinly sliced

1 (10.5-oz [294-g]) can beef consommé*

2 tbsp (30 ml) cooking sherry

1 tbsp (8 g) cornstarch

1 tsp thyme

2 lb (910 g) frozen green beans, thawed

1½ cups (180 g) shredded Swiss cheese, divided

3 cups (150 g) Croutons* (page 190)

Use gluten-free beef consommé or Beef Broth (page 192) and gluten-free croutons to make this recipe gluten-free.

Melt the butter in a large skillet. Add the onions and cook over medium heat for 10 minutes, or until the onions are tender and brown. If the onions appear to be getting too crisp, lower the heat.

Preheat the oven to 400°F (200°C, or gas mark 6). Grease a 9 x 13-inch (23 x 33-cm) baking pan.

Push the onions to the side of the pan and add the beef consommé, sherry and cornstarch. Use a whisk to blend the cornstarch into the liquid. Add the thyme and green beans. Cook over medium heat until the sauce thickens.

Spoon the green beans and onions into the prepared pan.

Sprinkle the green beans with ¾ cup (90 g) shredded cheese. Place the croutons on top of the cheese. Press them down, so they are firmly embedded in the casserole. Then sprinkle the remaining ¾ cup (90 g) cheese on top of the croutons.

Bake for 30 minutes.

PREP-AHEAD TIP: Save time by slicing the onions 2 or 3 days in advance and storing them in a sealed container in the refrigerator. Make the croutons 2 or 3 days in advance and store them in a sealed container or resealable bag in a cool, dry location.

You can also assemble this casserole the night before, cover the dish with a lid or foil, and store in the refrigerator overnight.

SEASONED POTATO WEDGES

Since my youngest son would like to live on French fries, I prefer to make homemade potato wedges with potatoes from my garden. Although they are not as healthy as some of the other vegetable dishes in this chapter, I at least know the growing conditions of the potatoes and can ensure they are not exposed to any unwanted chemicals.

4 russet potatoes

2 tbsp (30 ml) olive oil

1 tbsp (8 g) garlic powder

1 tbsp (8 g) onion powder

1 tbsp (8 g) smoked paprika

1 tsp chili powder

1 tsp Seasoned Salt* (page 183)

Use gluten-free Seasoned Salt to make this dish gluten-free.

Preheat the oven to 425°F (220°C, or gas mark 7).

Wash the potatoes and remove any eyes, but do not peel. Cut the potatoes in half, then cut each half into 8 wedges.

Place the potato wedges in a large bowl. Drizzle the oil over the potatoes, then toss to coat. Sprinkle the spices over the potatoes, then toss until evenly coated.

Place the potato wedges on the baking sheet so that one cut side is on the tray.

Bake for 20 minutes in the lower third of the oven. Flip the potato wedges to the other cut side and bake for another 20 minutes, or until the outside is crisp and the inside is tender.

BATCH-COOKING TIP: Potato wedges do take a while to cook. If you wish, you can make a double or triple batch. After roasting the potato wedges, freeze the extras on a baking sheet in the freezer. Once they are frozen, transfer them to a large freezer bag. When you want to cook the frozen fries, preheat the oven to 425°F (220°C, or gas mark 7). Spread the fries out on a baking sheet and bake for 15 to 20 minutes.

BAKED MASHED POTATOES

I have discovered that it is easier to make lump-free mashed potatoes if I bake the potatoes rather than boil cut-up potatoes. For fancier dinners, I spoon the mashed potatoes back into the potato skins and bake them again to create twice-baked potatoes.

---

4 russet potatoes

¼ cup (56 g) butter

½ cup (120 ml) milk

Seasoned Salt* (page 183) and pepper to taste

* Use gluten-free Seasoned Salt to make this dish gluten-free.

Preheat the oven to 400°F (200°C, or gas mark 6). Wash the potatoes and remove any eyes. Pierce the potatoes with a fork.

Bake for 1 hour, or until the potatoes are fork-tender.

If you want to use the potato skins in another recipe, cut an oval into the top of the potato. Pull off the top and scoop out the inside of the potato.

Mash the potatoes with a potato masher.

Add the butter, milk and a few pinches of salt and pepper to the potatoes and whip the ingredients with a fork or a hand mixer.

To Make Twice-Baked Potatoes

If you wish, you can top the twice-baked potatoes with paprika, chives, crumbled bacon, cheese or a combination of these ingredients. It only takes a few sprinkles of paprika to add color. If you choose to use chives, cheese or bacon, you will want to plan on 1 to 2 teaspoons per potato.

Follow the steps above to make the mashed potatoes. When baking the mashed potatoes again inside the potato skins, you want the mashed potatoes to be on the moist side. If they seem dry, add a little more milk and mix again.

Spoon the mashed potatoes back into the potatoes. Put enough in that it mounds and protrudes a bit from the top of the potato skin. (If you make these the day before your dinner, you can place your potatoes in a baking dish, cover it and refrigerate overnight. You will need to add a few minutes to the baking time.)

Sprinkle the potatoes with paprika, chives, bacon crumbles or cheese. Bake for 18 to 22 minutes, or until the insides are warm and the tops are slightly browned.

PREP-AHEAD TIP: As with sweet potatoes, it is quite convenient to bake the potatoes 1 or 2 days in advance and then use them to make mashed potatoes.

ORANGE GINGER SNAP PEAS

For a long time, I only served snap peas raw either on a vegetable platter with a dip or in a salad. One day I was searching the refrigerator for a green vegetable to serve as a side dish and only came up with snap peas. I decided to sauté them in some orange juice and we discovered a whole new way to enjoy these tasty veggies.

3 cups (225 g) sugar snap peas

⅓ cup (80 ml) orange juice

1 tsp cornstarch

2 tsp (6 g) grated ginger

1 tbsp (15 ml) olive oil

2 tsp (6 g) sesame seeds

Remove the stem end and the string from the snap peas.

In a small bowl, whisk together the orange juice and cornstarch. Add the ginger and oil to the orange juice mixture; stir to combine.

Pour the orange juice mixture into a skillet. Add the snap peas and toss to coat.

Cook the snap peas over medium-high heat for 5 minutes.

Sprinkle the sesame seeds over the snap peas and toss to coat. Cook for 1 more minute, or until the snap peas are crisp-tender.

PREP-AHEAD TIP: This dish comes together quickly and it also holds up well. If you wish, you can cook the Orange Ginger Snap Peas 2 or 3 days in advance and then reheat them over low heat before serving.

LEMON PEPPER ZUCCHINI

This is a quick and easy vegetable recipe. It comes together in less than 10 minutes, making it an ideal side dish on busy weeknights. I don't know anyone who doesn't have zucchini on hand during the summer, but if for some reason one of your neighbors hasn't dropped off a bag of zucchinis on your porch, you can substitute any summer squash in this recipe.

1 tbsp (14 g) butter

1 tbsp (15 ml) olive oil

1 tbsp (15 ml) lemon juice

4 small zucchinis, sliced ¼-inch (6-mm) thick

½ tsp Seasoned Salt* (page 183)

¼ tsp coarsely ground pepper

* Use gluten-free Seasoned Salt to make this dish gluten-free.

Melt the butter in a skillet. Add the oil and lemon juice and stir to blend.

Add the zucchini slices to the skillet. Toss to coat. Sprinkle the zucchini with the seasoned salt and pepper and toss again.

Cook over medium-high heat for 7 minutes, or until the zucchini is fork-tender.

PREP-AHEAD TIP: Save time by juicing your lemon in advance and store the juice in a sealed container in the refrigerator for a week or in the freezer for up to 4 months. You can also slice the zucchini 1 or 2 days in advance and store in a resealable plastic bag in the refrigerator.

SPICY ASIAN YELLOW SQUASH

I love yellow squash, especially straight-neck yellow squash. It has a very mild taste, which allows it to pick up the flavors of the other ingredients in the dish. I add a little bit of kick to this side dish by combining crushed red pepper flakes with traditional Asian flavors.

The trick to making delicious squash recipes is to use small squash. The larger the squash, the more seeds you have to deal with. If you use small summer squash, the seeds haven't fully developed yet, so the squash is firmer and more pleasant to cook with.

---

1 tbsp (15 ml) sesame oil

2 tbsp (30 ml) soy sauce*

2 tbsp (30 ml) rice vinegar

1 tsp sugar

3 or 4 small yellow squash, sliced ¼-inch (6-mm) thick

¼ tsp crushed red pepper flakes

* Substitute gluten-free soy sauce to make this recipe gluten-free.

Add the oil, soy sauce, vinegar and sugar to a hot skillet. Stir over medium heat until the sugar is dissolved.

Add the yellow squash and toss to coat. Sprinkle the red pepper flakes over the squash and toss one more time.

Cook over medium-high heat for 7 minute, or until the squash is fork-tender.

PREP-AHEAD TIP: You can slice the yellow squash 1 or 2 days in advance and store in a resealable plastic bag in the refrigerator.

ROASTED ORANGE GINGER BEETS

When I buy beets at the store, I buy whole beets with the leaves still attached. The leaves are edible and make a great addition to any salad. After I cook the beets, I serve them over a bed of greens that includes the torn-up beet leaves. The trick to cooking beets quickly is to cut them really thin and to make your slices as uniform as possible so they cook in the same amount of time.

¾ cup (180 ml) orange juice

3 tbsp (45 ml) honey

1 tbsp (8 g) grated ginger

¾ tsp ground cinnamon

4 medium beets, peeled and thinly sliced

Preheat the oven to 450°F (230°C, or gas mark 8). Line a baking sheet with foil.

In a large bowl, combine the orange juice, honey and spices. Add the beet slices and stir to coat.

Place the beet slices on the lined baking sheet. Reserve the leftover orange ginger sauce. Bake for 15 minutes.

Drizzle the reserved orange ginger sauce over the beets. Then turn the beets over and bake for 10 minutes longer, or until the beets are tender.

PREP-AHEAD Tip: You can wash and slice the beets a day or two in advance. Store the cut beets in a lidded container or a plastic bag with a moistened paper towel to keep them from drying out.

FIESTA CORN WITH BLACK BEANS

The colorful peppers and bright yellow corn make this dish look like confetti. Since I want this dish to remain bright and colorful, I rinse the black beans before adding them to the pan, so the liquid from the beans doesn't muddy the color of the dish.

I pair this with Southwestern entrées and use it in place of refried beans.

1 tbsp (15 ml) olive oil

½ cup (80 g) diced red onion

½ cup (75 g) diced green bell pepper

½ cup (75 g) diced red bell pepper

2 cups (260 g) frozen sweet corn, thawed

1¾ cups (438 g) black beans, rinsed

2 tsp (6 g) Taco Seasoning Mix* (page 184)

1 to 2 tbsp (15 to 30 ml) water, if needed

Use gluten-free Taco Seasoning Mix to make this dish gluten-free.

Heat the oil in a skillet or frying pan. Add the diced onion and bell peppers. Sauté over medium-high heat for 5 minutes, or until the onion is tender.

Add the corn, black beans and taco seasoning to the skillet. Stir to combine with the onion and peppers and ensure the taco seasoning is evenly distributed.

Continue cooking over medium heat for 5 minutes, or until the corn and beans are heated through. If the pan starts to dry out, add a little water, 1 tablespoon (15 ml) at a time.

PREP-AHEAD Tip: You can dice the onion and peppers ahead of time and store them in sealed containers for 2 to 3 days in the refrigerator or up to 3 months in the freezer.

Serves: 6

BROILED CHIPOTLE SWEET POTATOES

These are quite spicy, but the sweet potato helps offset the heat. If you wish, you can cut the spices in half and add a tablespoon (15 ml) of honey to make a milder variation: Honey Chipotle Sweet Potatoes.

3 large sweet potatoes

2 tbsp (30 ml) olive oil

1 tbsp (8 g) Chipotle Seasoning Mix* (page 185)

* Use gluten-free Chipotle Seasoning Mix to make this gluten-free.

Preheat the oven to broil. Cover your broiling pan with foil if you wish to make cleanup easier.

Wash, dry and cut any eyes from the sweet potatoes, but do not peel.

Cut the sweet potatoes into bite-size pieces and place them on the broiling pan.

Drizzle the olive oil over the sweet potatoes and toss to coat. Sprinkle the spice mix over the sweet potatoes and toss until the pieces are well covered with the spice mix.

Place the pan in the oven and broil for 15 minutes, or until the sweet potatoes are fork-tender. Use a spatula to flip the sweet potatoes every 5 minutes while cooking to prevent burning.

PREP-AHEAD Tip: You can reduce the prep time by cutting the sweet potatoes a day or two in advance. Store the sweet potato pieces in a bowl and cover with water. Pat the sweet potato pieces dry before using them in the recipe.

Frugal Pantry Staples

If you look at how much your groceries cost per pound, you may find that convenience spice mixes are the most expensive item you buy. You may have thought you got a good deal when you picked up that 1¼-ounce (35-g) taco seasoning packet on sale for 99 cents, but if you do the math, that equals $12.67 per pound (455 g). The cost of little seasoning packets and convenience foods adds up fast. Many of them are made with common pantry staples, so you can save money by making your own homemade spice mixes instead of buying prepackaged mixes.

The bulk food section is not just for rice and beans. Some grocery stores sell spices in bulk, allowing you to buy as little or as much as you wish at significant savings compared with those same ingredients in the spice aisle. You can also save on spices by shopping for them at ethnic food markets.

In this section I include recipes for commonly used spice mixes as well as salad dressings, barbecue sauce, spaghetti sauce and enchilada sauce. I also include directions for making bread crumbs, croutons and homemade broths.

CAJUN SEASONING MIX

Makes: ¾ cup (64 g)

My husband and kids enjoy this Cajun Seasoning Mix so much that they will eat just about anything I season it with—even vegetables! Although it contains come cayenne pepper, it doesn't overpower the other spices in the mix.

Used in Cajun-Spiced Cauliflower (page 154), Cajun Red Beans and Rice Wraps (page 145), Cajun Pulled Pork Wraps (page 70) and Cajun Chicken and Pasta (page 43).

2 tbsp (36 g) salt

2 tbsp (16 g) garlic powder

2 tbsp (16 g) smoked paprika

2 tbsp (16 g) onion powder

1 tbsp (8 g) cayenne pepper

1 tbsp (8 g) ground black pepper

1 tbsp (3 g) dried oregano

1 tbsp (3 g) dried thyme

1½ tsp (1.5 g) red pepper flakes (optional)

Combine the spices in a small bowl. Stir until thoroughly mixed.

Store in an airtight container.

SEASONED SALT

Makes: ½ cup (14 g)

I use this Seasoned Salt recipe in almost every savory dish I make. It enhances the flavors of the dishes without making them too salty. Used in Chicken Marsala Pizza (page 16), Skillet Mac & Cheese (page 50), Baked Meatballs (page 107) and Seasoned Potato Wedges (page 170).

¼ cup (72 g) sea salt

2 tbsp (1.5 g) dried parsley

1 tsp onion powder

1 tsp garlic powder

½ tsp oregano

½ tsp rosemary

½ tsp thyme

½ tsp sage

½ tsp basil

½ tsp marjoram

Place all ingredients in a food processor and chop until smooth and blended.

Let the spices settle, then remove from the food processor and store in an airtight container.

Use as called for in recipes.

TACO SEASONING MIX

Makes: ⅓ cup (43 g)

Store-bought taco seasoning mix often contains fillers that are not necessary to the flavor. The great thing about making your own seasoning mixes is that you can tailor them to your taste. Use this as a guide, but feel free to experiment to create your own unique blend.

Used in White Bean and Chicken Ranch Tacos (page 30), Chicken Fajita Pizza with a Cornmeal Crust (page 20), Lentil and Rice Tacos (page 134), 15-Minute Refried Black Beans (page 135), Fiesta Corn with Black Beans (page 178), Southwest Rice Salad with Avocado (page 131), Fajita Frittata (page 91), Southwestern Sloppy Joes (page 83), Southwest Three-Bean Salad (page 127), Black Bean and Mushroom Enchiladas (page 120) and Black Bean and Sweet Potato Burritos (page 132).

1½ tbsp (12 g) chili powder

1½ tbsp (12 g) cumin

1 tbsp (8 g) paprika (I prefer smoked paprika)

1 tbsp (8 g) garlic powder

1 tbsp (8 g) onion powder

1 tsp dried cilantro

⅛ tsp cayenne pepper (optional)

In a small bowl, mix all the ingredients together.

Store in an airtight container for up to 6 months.

ITALIAN SEASONING MIX

Makes: ¼ cup (20 g)

I keep homemade Italian Seasoning Mix on hand because it is a quick and easy way to add all of the traditional Italian spices to soups and sauces with one measuring spoon.

Used in Cabbage Roll Casserole (page 92), Baked Italian Spring Rolls (page 86), Spaghetti Sauce (page 188) and Swiss Steak Stew (page 101).

2 tbsp (6 g) oregano

2 tbsp (6 g) basil

2 tbsp (1.5 g) parsley

2 tsp (6 g) garlic powder

1 tsp onion powder

½ tsp thyme

½ tsp rosemary

In a small bowl, combine all of the ingredients. Mix well.

Store in an airtight container for up to 6 months.

PUMPKIN PIE SPICE MIX

Makes:
¼ cup
(30 g)

Don't limit the delicious flavors of pumpkin pie spice to desserts! I like to use pumpkin pie spice to make already sweet vegetables like carrots, parsnips and sweet potatoes more appealing to my kids.

Used in Pumpkin Pie–Spiced Parsnip Fries (page 163) and Jamaican Jerk Pork Stuffed Zucchini (page 75).

2 tbsp (16 g) cinnamon

2 tsp (6 g) nutmeg

2 tsp (6 g) ground ginger

1 tsp ground cloves

Add the spices to a spice jar. Put the lid on and shake vigorously to mix.

Store in a lidded container in a cool, dark place.

CHIPOTLE SEASONING MIX

Makes:
6 tbsp
(48 g)

Chipotle Seasoning Mix provides a delicious, spicier and hotter alternative to Taco Seasoning Mix (page 184) in a variety of recipes.

Used in Broiled Chipotle Sweet Potatoes (page 181) and Chipotle Pulled Pork Tacos (page 49).

1 tbsp (8 g) ground chipotle chile pepper

1 tbsp (8 g) garlic powder

1 tbsp (8 g) onion powder

1 tbsp (8 g) ground coriander

2 tsp (6 g) paprika (smoked paprika if available)

1 tsp black pepper

1 tsp ground cumin

1 tsp oregano (Mexican oregano if available)

½ tsp Seasoned Salt* (page 183)

½ tsp cayenne pepper

Add all the spices to a spice jar and shake to mix thoroughly.

Store in an airtight container for up to 6 months.

* Use gluten-free Seasoned Salt to make this gluten-free.

POULTRY SEASONING MIX

Makes:
¼ cup
(10 g)

I keep this Poultry Seasoning Mix on hand so I can sprinkle the spices traditionally used on poultry as easily as I can salt and pepper a chicken before roasting it. If there is a combination of spices you find yourself using over and over again, it simplifies your meal prep to make your own seasoning mix and pull out one jar instead of five or six.

Used on roast chicken (page 12).

1 tbsp (2 g) marjoram

1 tbsp (2 g) ground sage

1 tbsp (2 g) thyme

2 tsp (1.5 g) rosemary

2 tsp (1 g) parsley

½ tsp celery seed

In a small bowl, mix all of the spices together.

Store in an airtight container in a cool, dry location.

Shake before using, as the spices will settle.

ITALIAN SALAD DRESSING

Makes:
2 cups
(470 ml)

The great thing about making your own salad dressing is you can tailor it to your taste. My family prefers this dressing with balsamic vinegar, but feel free to experiment with other vinegars that you have on hand.

Used in Italian Artichoke Hearts (page 157), Italian Rice Salad with Artichoke Hearts (page 140) and Ratatouille Rice Skillet (page 143).

1 cup (235 ml) olive oil

¾ cup (180 ml) balsamic vinegar

2 tbsp (30 ml) water

1 tbsp (12 g) sugar

1 tbsp (2 g) dried oregano

1½ tsp (3 g) garlic powder

1½ tsp (3 g) onion powder

½ tsp dried thyme

½ tsp dried basil

¼ tsp ground black pepper

⅛ tsp salt

Place all the ingredients in a cruet or jar with a lid.

Shake well to blend the ingredients.

Store in the refrigerator for up to a week.

RANCH SALAD DRESSING

This tangy ranch dressing is packed with herbs and spices. This recipe uses milk and lemon juice in place of buttermilk, since I rarely have buttermilk on hand. However, if you have buttermilk, substitute it for the milk and lemon juice and skip the first step.

Used in White Bean and Chicken Ranch Tacos (page 30), Southwest Rice Salad with Avocado (page 131) and Buffalo Ranch Chicken Squash Boats (page 15).

1 tbsp (15 ml) lemon juice

½ cup (120 ml) milk

¾ cup (180 g) sour cream

1 tbsp (2 g) dried parsley

1 tsp onion powder

¾ tsp garlic powder

½ tsp dill weed

½ tsp dried basil

½ tsp Seasoned Salt* (page 183)

¼ tsp ground mustard

¼ tsp coarsely ground pepper

Use gluten-free Seasoned Salt to make this gluten-free.

In a small cup, add the lemon juice to the milk and let it sit for 5 minutes.

In a small bowl, combine the sour cream and spices. Mix well to combine.

Add the milk to the sour cream mixture and blend well.

Refrigerate in an airtight container for 1 to 2 hours before using.

Keeps in the refrigerator for up to 3 days.

ENCHILADA SAUCE

Makes: 5½ cups (1295 ml)

This recipe makes a fairly mild enchilada sauce, but if you want even less heat reduce the cayenne pepper. If after making this sauce if it isn't hot enough for you, add more cayenne pepper a pinch at a time until you achieve the desired heat. You can make this enchilada sauce ahead of time and store it in the refrigerator for 4 or 5 days or in the freezer for up to 3 months.

Used in Black Bean and Mushroom Enchiladas (page 120) and Enchilada Casserole (page 104).

3 cups (705 ml) Vegetable Broth *
(page 193)

2 cups (470 ml) tomato sauce

⅓ cup (40 g) chili powder

¼ cup (32 g) cornstarch

2 tbsp (30 ml) olive oil

1 tsp garlic powder

1 tsp onion powder

1 tsp ground cumin

1 tsp dried oregano

¼ tsp cayenne pepper

Place all of the ingredients in a saucepan over medium-high heat. Cook the sauce until it boils. Reduce the heat and simmer until it thickens.

Use in enchilada recipes as called for. Store any unused portion in the refrigerator for 4 or 5 days or in the freezer for up to 3 months.

* Use gluten-free Vegetable Broth to make this sauce gluten-free.

SPAGHETTI SAUCE

Makes: 3½ cups (735 ml)

There is no reason to buy premade spaghetti sauce when you probably have all the ingredients needed to make it in your pantry. You can double or triple this recipe and then freeze the sauce in usable portions to always have some readily available.

Used Chicken Parmesan Pasta Bake (page 24), as a dipping sauce with Baked Italian Spring Rolls (page 86) and to make spaghetti with meatballs (page 107).

1 tbsp (15 ml) olive oil

½ cup (80 g) diced onion

4 cloves garlic, minced

1¾ cups (315 g) diced tomatoes or 1 (14.5-oz [406-g]) can diced tomatoes

1¾ cups (430 g) tomato sauce or 1 (15 oz [425 g]) can tomato sauce

1 tbsp (12 g) sugar

1 tbsp (6 g) Italian Seasoning Mix*
(page 184)

Add the olive oil, onion and garlic to a large saucepan. Sauté for 5 minutes, or until the onions are tender.

Add the tomatoes, tomato sauce, sugar and Italian Seasoning Mix. Stir to fully incorporate the spices.

Cook over medium-high heat until it reaches a boil. Then lower the temperature and simmer uncovered for at least 15 minutes.

* Use gluten-free Italian Seasoning Mix to make this sauce gluten-free.

BARBECUE SAUCE

This sweet and tangy barbecue sauce is thick and has a mild smoky flavor.

Used in Barbecue Beef Pasta Skillet (page 98) and Barbecue Pulled Pork Stuffed Sweet Potatoes (page 68).

1¾ cups (430 ml) or 1 (15-oz [430-ml]) can tomato sauce

2 tbsp (30 ml) apple cider vinegar

¼ cup (55 g) brown sugar

2 tbsp (30 ml) maple syrup

2 tbsp (30 ml) Worcestershire sauce*

1 tbsp (8 g) smoked paprika

2 tsp (4 g) garlic powder

2 tsp (4 g) onion powder

1½ tsp (4 g) mustard powder

1 tsp chili powder

½ tsp ground cinnamon

* Use gluten-free Worcestershire sauce to make this sauce gluten-free.

Combine all of the ingredients in a medium saucepan. Cook over medium-high heat until the sauce reaches a boil.

Reduce the heat and simmer for 15 minutes.

Store the sauce in the refrigerator for 1 week or the freezer for up to 3 months.

BREAD CRUMBS

I save all the crusts, leftover rolls and stale bread and freeze it. It is easier to grate frozen bread and makes it easy to turn something that would otherwise be tossed out into usable bread crumbs for recipes.

Plain bread crumbs used in Chicken Cordon Bleu Rice Bake (page 29).

Enough frozen bread* to equal 1 cup (100 g) of crumbs

If making Italian bread crumbs, use 2½ tsp (6 g) Italian Seasoning Mix* (page 184)

Use gluten-free bread and gluten-free Italian Seasoning Mix to make gluten-free bread crumbs.

Preheat the oven to 350°F (180°C, or gas mark 4).

Grate the frozen bread over a small bowl. Don't worry if you have a few pieces that are a little bigger.

Add spices to the bread crumbs if you are making Italian bread crumbs and mix well.

Spread the crumbs over a large cookie sheet and bake for 10 minutes, or until the crumbs are dry and slightly brown.

CROUTONS

You can use whatever spices you wish when making croutons. I usually use garlic powder and onion powder. I sometimes add parsley to give it a spot of color and often choose a few spices that will accompany the recipe that I will be using the croutons in.

Used in French Onion Green Bean Casserole (page 169) and Bierock Soup (page 84).

8 to 10 pieces bread*

¼ cup (60 ml) olive oil

1 tsp garlic powder

1 tsp onion powder

1 tsp thyme or sage (optional)

1 tsp parsley (optional)

Use gluten-free bread to make gluten-free croutons.

Preheat the oven to 450°F (230°C, or gas mark 8).

Place your pieces of bread on a large ungreased baking sheet.

Brush one side of the bread with olive oil and dust with garlic powder, onion powder, thyme and parsley.

Flip the bread over and repeat.

Using a pizza cutter, cut the bread into bite-size pieces.

Bake for 5 to 8 minutes, or until they are toasty brown, tossing the croutons every 2 to 3 minutes.

Leave the croutons on the baking sheet to cool and then store them in an airtight container.

CHICKEN BROTH

Makes:
8 cups
(1880 ml)

Save the bones when you batch cook chickens and use them to make broth. If you don't have time to make the broth right away, you can freeze the bones and use them later. If you have a large enough pot, slow cooker or pressure cooker, you can double this recipe. Used in Asian Chicken and Rice Soup (page 23), Chicken Paprikash (page 39) and White Chili with Rice (page 57).

1 chicken carcass

2 stalks celery, coarsely chopped

2 large carrots, coarsely chopped

1 medium yellow onion, quartered

2 cloves garlic, coarsely chopped

1 tsp apple cider vinegar (optional)

1 bay leaf (optional)

8 cups (1880 ml) water

Add the chicken carcass to a slow cooker, pressure cooker or large stockpot.

Add the celery, carrots, onion, garlic, vinegar and bay leaf to the chicken.

Pour the water over the chicken bones and cook according to the directions below.

Slow Cooker Cooking Time

Cook on high for 2 hours. Reduce the heat to low and cook for 10 to 12 hours.

Pressure Cooker Cooking Time

Cover and bring to high pressure. Cook for 30 minutes. Allow the pressure to release naturally, which should take about 25 minutes.

Stove Top Cooking Time

Cook over high heat until it begins to boil. Lower the heat, cover and simmer for 2 hours.

Place a colander over a bowl and strain the liquid. Save any bits of meat to use later in recipes, but discard the bones and vegetables.

Cool the broth in the refrigerator, then scoop off any fat that gathers at the top. If you wish you can strain the broth one more time.

The broth can be refrigerated for up to 4 or 5 days. You can ladle the broth into freezer-safe containers and freeze it for up to 4 months.

BEEF BROTH

Save the bones from your roasts and use them to make broth. It will probably take two to four roasts before you have enough bones to make broth. Add the leftover bones to a sealable bag and store in the freezer until you have 3 to 4 pounds (1365 to 1820 g) of bones. Used in Bierock Soup (page 84), Skillet Stroganoff (page 85), Cottage Pie (page 99), Dutch Oven Borscht Pasta Bake (page 100) and Swiss Steak Stew (page 101).

---

3 to 4 lb (1365 to 1820 g) beef bones

2 stalks celery, coarsely chopped

2 large carrots, coarsely chopped

1 large yellow onion, quartered

2 cloves garlic, coarsely chopped

1 tsp apple cider vinegar (optional)

1 bay leaf (optional)

1 tsp dried thyme (optional)

3 or 4 whole peppercorns

8 cups (1880 ml) water

Add the beef bones to a slow cooker, pressure cooker or large stockpot.

Add the celery, carrots, onion, garlic, vinegar, bay leaf, thyme and peppercorns to the bones.

Pour the water over the bones and vegetables and cook according to the directions below.

Slow Cooker Cooking Time

Cook on high for 2 hours. Reduce the heat to low and cook for 10 to 12 hours.

Pressure Cooker Cooking Time

Cover and bring to high pressure. Cook for 1 hour. Allow the pressure to release naturally, which should take about 30 minutes.

Stove Top Cooking Time

Cook over high heat until it begins to boil. Lower the heat, cover and simmer for 3½ to 4 hours.

Place a colander over a bowl and strain the liquid. Save any bits of meat to use later in recipes, but discard the bones and vegetables.

Cool the broth in the refrigerator, then scoop off any fat that gathers at the top. If you wish you can strain the broth one more time.

The broth can be refrigerated for up to 4 or 5 days. You can ladle the broth into freezer-safe containers and freeze it for up to 4 months.

VEGETABLE BROTH

Makes: 8 cups (1880 ml)

I have listed ingredients for vegetable broth, but these are just guidelines. Feel free to use the equivalent in vegetables scraps if you wish. I collect carrot peels, celery tops and onion skins as I am prepping vegetables for other recipes and keep them in the freezer to use as the base for my vegetable broth. If you are using fresh vegetables, don't bother peeling them. Just wash the vegetables and coarsely chop them before adding them to the pot. Used in Alfredo Sauce (page 26), Honey Lemon Pork and Broccoli (page 53), White Bean and Ham Soup with Spinach (page 60), Potato, Ham and Corn Chowder (page 63), Tuscan White Bean and Acorn Squash Soup (page 123) and Three Bean Minestrone Soup (page 119).

3 stalks celery, coarsely chopped

3 large carrots, coarsely chopped

2 medium yellow onions, quartered

2 cloves garlic, coarsely chopped

1 large potato, coarsely chopped

1 bay leaf (optional)

½ tsp thyme (optional)

½ tsp basil (optional)

8 cups (1880 ml) water

Add the celery, carrots, onion, garlic, potato, bay leaf, thyme and basil to a slow cooker, pressure cooker or large stockpot.

Pour the water over the vegetables and cook according to the directions below.

Slow Cooker Cooking Time

Cook on low for 8 hours.

Pressure Cooker Cooking Time

Cover and bring to high pressure. Cook for 10 minutes. Allow the pressure to release naturally, which should take about 10 minutes.

Stove Top Cooking Time

Cook over high heat until it begins to boil. Lower the heat, cover and simmer for 1 hour.

Place a colander over a bowl and strain the liquid. Discard the vegetables.

The broth can be refrigerated for up to 4 or 5 days. You can ladle the broth into freezer-safe containers and freeze it for up to 4 months.

ACKNOWLEDGMENTS

Thank you to the Page Street Publishing team for sharing your insights and guiding me through the process of writing this book. Will and Marissa, thank you for listening to my ideas and allowing me to run with them.

Chris Holloman, thank you for capturing my vision and the flavors of my recipes in your pictures.

I am grateful to Shirley Braden of Gluten Free Easily for answering my questions about gluten-free food substitutions. Any errors are my own.

Thank you to my friends and neighbors who served as taste testers, dish washers and child wranglers. Bev, Colleen, Marc, Nathan, Julia, Laura, Pauline, Maralee, Mark, Kate and Glenna, your feedback was invaluable. A heartfelt thanks to Laura for taking such good care of Andrew and allowing me to concentrate on preparing recipes during the photo shoots.

I appreciate the encouragement and support I have received from my blogging friends and the foodie community. Taylor, Melissa, Dana and Kim, thank you for sharing your feedback and ideas.

I am grateful for my team at Premeditated Leftovers. Christine, Patricia, Erin, Katie F., Emily, Jody, Grant, Katie H., Stacy, Derrick and Tatanisha, I appreciate your help in keeping my blog up and running while I was busy in the kitchen.

Thanks to my in-laws, Pat, Russ and the Leglers, for accommodating my photo shoots during your vacation and being adventurous enough to enter "the splash-zone" and serve as taste testers. A special thanks to my mother-in-law, Pat, for welcoming me to the family by sharing her family recipes.

I am thankful to my parents for allowing me free range in the kitchen from a young age and for their encouragement to continue creating recipes despite a couple of epic mishaps.

A special thanks to my sister, Corriedawn, for extending her visit to help with a photo shoot and for always encouraging me to stretch beyond my comfort zone.

A huge thank-you to my family for their willingness to serve as my sous chefs, dish washers and most important, guinea pigs for my recipes.

Patricia, Grant and Andrew, I appreciate your willingness to "speed date food" as I experiment with ingredients and to provide your honest, and often entertaining, feedback.

Pete, thank you for your encouragement, for serving as my "sous shopper" and for diving into the fray as soon as you walked in the door, providing me with much-needed time to write.

ABOUT THE AUTHOR

Alea Milham is the founder of Premeditated Leftovers, where she shares simple recipes made with whole foods, practical shopping tips, time-saving techniques and meal-planning strategies. Alea also shares tips for minimizing food waste, so more of the food that is purchased ends up on the table.

While volunteering as a budget counselor, Alea recognized that food is the element of most people's budgets where they have the greatest control. She set out to develop low-cost recipes from scratch, so her readers could create delicious meals on a limited budget. She realizes that eating well while spending less is about more than just creating recipes using inexpensive ingredients; it's about creatively combining ingredients so you don't feel deprived and are inspired to stick to your budget.

Alea lives on 2 acres in the high desert with her husband, children and small menagerie. Her favorite hobby, gardening, is a frugal source of organic produce for her recipes.

INDEX